The Gift of Faith

Carol Goodman

Carol Goodman

i

THE GIFT OF FAITH

DEDICATION

I write this story so my children, grandchildren and great grandchildren will have the history I want them to know about me and my family. The most important part of my life was my experiences and the wisdom I gained with age. I always believed in God but I didn't always follow him. He gave me the gift of Faith. He has brought me through many storms and I have become a better person because of them.

In order for God to take you to another place
He must first move you from where you are.

The move often seems like a disaster but it's only
The creaking and groaning of a reluctant door.

Author Unknown

CAROL GOODMAN

Elmer   Mable
Saunders

Elmer Saunders & Mabel Lear
Married 1914
Helen-Emmet-Willard-Mildred-Wilma-Frank-Judy

Willard Saunders & Faye Bunner
Married 1941
Carol-Sharon

Carol Saunders & Dempsey Billey
Married 1961
Michelle-Denise

Carol Billey & Gill Goodman
Married 1968
Debra-Jill

Robert Bunner & Rosa Faye Parker
Married 1915
Robert-Lois-Faye

Rosa Faye Parker & Charles Wakefield
Married 1927
June-Charles

CONTENTS

CAROL GOODMAN

CHAPTER 1
BEGINNINGS

My name is Carol Elaine Saunders and I was born August 20, 1942 in Cripple Creek, Colorado, a town high in the mountains. It was a little over 9000 feet above sea level.

It was the site of a gold mining boom that began at the beginning of the 1900's. My great-grandfather, Peter Saunders, was a shoemaker from England who immigrated to find his fortune mining gold. This was mostly hard rock mining, where mining companies sunk shafts deep underground and extracted the ore from the rock. It was a hard life. Just imagine an average

snowfall of 54" a year and being so high in the mountains it didn't melt very quickly. How do you get fresh vegetables? Summers were short and when they grew vegetables, they were canned so the family would have vegetables during the winter. The men would hunt and provide meat for the season. They would store the meat in a frozen shed out back.

Peter's son, Elmer—my grandfather—also became a miner, as did most of the men in the family, including my own father, Willard Llewellyn Saunders (better known as Lou).

Mabln, Helen, Lou, Elmer
Judy Wilma, Mildred, Frank,
Earl & Bill

Bud out hunting

Dad was one of seven brothers and sisters. He was the third oldest child and one of the older boys. They had to learn how to survive in the mining town of Cripple Creek, with everyone contributing to keep the family afloat. He learned to cook stews and soup just like the girls and figured out how to fix things when they broke.

There were wild donkeys in the mountains that were used originally in the mines to haul the tram cars. Donkeys wandered free throughout the town as well. My dad and his siblings trained two of the donkeys— named Dick and Prince— and rode them whenever they had time.

When dad was in junior high School his father, Elmer, had a bad accident when a mine caved in. Both of his legs were broken and he could no longer work. There was no such thing as Social Security, or disability to take care of families in this situation. Dad and his siblings had to quit school and go to work to help support the

family. The boys started working in the mines at a very young age, about fifteen, and the girls went to work waitressing or house-keeping.

My dad told stories of using canaries in the mines. They would take the canaries in the cages down into the mineshaft

and tunnels. When the birds stopped singing the miners knew it usually meant there was not enough oxygen deep in the mine, and they all got out.

Lois, Rosa Faye, Cora Faye, Mr. Wakefield, Robert
The children above were the Bunner Family

My mother, Cora Faye Bunner, was one of five children. Her parents, Rosa Faye and Robert Bunner, had three children. Mom's brother Robert was born in 1916, her sister Lois was born in 1918 and after a break of seven years, my mother was born in 1925. Her father, Robert Bunner, died suddenly of a stroke shortly after she was born. Rosa Faye depended on her mother to support herself and three small children.

Rosa Faye remarried to a man named Charles Wakefield some time later. With him she had two more children. June was born about 1929, and a brother Charles born in 1931. When my mother was only eight years old, Rosa Faye died of cancer. Her stepfather, Charles, took off with June and little Charles, his biological children. Robert and Lois were already grown and gone by that time but my mother was left with her grandmother. It soon became apparent that the grandmother couldn't care for my mother either physically or financially, and so her brother Robert, newly married, tried to take Cora in. It was too much for them financially as well. Robert remembered their father had been a

June & Charles Wakefield

Mason so he got my mother placed in a Masonic Home for Orphans. Robert went to CC Camp and Lois married very young.

My mother therefore had an untraditional childhood. She lived in a two-story brick building with several other children and a few caregivers. She was never taught to cook or care for children. She told us stories of never having her own toys or dolls to play with. She really did not talk much about her time at the home.

She eventually went to Cripple Creek High School and played the clarinet in the orchestra. She also learned to play the piano and violin.

Mom was what I would call an inward person. She didn't express a lot of emotions or drama. She didn't feel sorry for herself. She was dedicated to my dad and his family and loved her children. She demanded that whatever job you were given would be done to the best of your abilities. If you did a sloppy

Cripple Creek Orchestra
Mom is the 5th person from the left in the back

job you were sent back to do it over again. I resented this until I grew up and saw the advantage of doing the best you can do in all situations.

When I had my children, she was always there to help. I really appreciated her input and care. She loved her grandchildren, but she just didn't live long enough for them to remember her.

Later in life she tried hard to find her younger half brother and sister. And because she was only eight years old when her mother died, she never knew where her mom was buried. She tried to find her mother's grave but never had any success. Her older brother and sister kept in contact and they carried on a relationship until she passed away. Mom died at the age of 51.

When the computer age came upon us, I started doing genealogy searches. I found June and Charles Wakefield and was able to actually go visit them at different times. One lived just outside of Denver and the other in upstate New York. I had pictures from my mom that they had never seen and I was able to share mom's story of trying to find them. Charles took me and my sister Sharon to our grandmother's grave site just outside of Denver. She had initially been buried in potter's field because their father had not finished paying for the burial. Charles and June waited until their father died so they had legal rights, and then paid to move her.

This picture was taken in 2006.

Carol & Sharon

CHAPTER 2
MY PARENTS AND ME

Cora Faye Bunner/Saunders & Lou Saunders

Mom and Dad met each other in 1940 at a community gathering. Dad was working in the mines and mother was in high school. Neither one of them graduated. They were married June 20, 1941. Mom moved right out of the Masonic Home and in with my father.

A few months later they discovered that I would be joining them. They were nervous about becoming parents. My mother had never been around babies and wasn't sure how to take care of them. Plus, it was an uncertain time for the country. The Great Depression had taken its toll on America, and the Japanese had just bombed Pearl Harbor, plunging the United States into World War II.

Whatever their apprehensions, I was born on August 20, 1942. Because my father had been raised with younger siblings, he was well equipped to teach Mom how to take care of me. Plus, upon their marriage, my mother joined the large Saunders family, and they helped her out. She often told me stories about my sickly infancy. With many cousins around I contracted all the childhood ailments—chicken pox, measles, and mumps—before the age of 3. I am not sure what the child-rearing protocol was in the early 40's, but I know Grandma Saunders knew how to take care of these things.

In 1943 my grandparents, Mabel and Elmer had to move to Rifle Colorado because Elmer had a lung disease called "consumption" and living in the high altitude made it hard for him to breathe.

That same year, my family moved to Leadville, Colorado. Dad had been offered a job at the Resurrection Mining Company. His wages for the year of 1944 were $3,000.19.

On January 18th of 1945, Dad was called to go into the U.S. Army to fight in World War II. He left for Fort Lear, Kansas on February 5th for Basic Training and then was sent to Camp Hood, Texas, on February 28th. Mom was able to go visit him at Camp Hood in April and spend three nights with him before he shipped out to Japan. She left me with my grandmother in Rifle, Colorado during her trip, and when my mother returned home we moved to Rifle to be near family. It was very hard for my mother.

The Christmas just after my third birthday, our church was having a Christmas play. Mother had taught me my lines for the play and was all excited to see me perform. Unfortunately the teacher forgot to call on me. Mother was quite upset and we left the church early, with her crying. As soon as we got home, the phone rang. It was my father. She was so excited to hear from him and instantly knew that God had sent her home to receive that phone call.

Even better, the purpose of the phone call was to tell Mom to catch a train to come to San Luis Obispo, California and join him. My Mom and I caught a train and moved to California in March of 1946. A few months later we moved to Monterey where my dad was discharged from Fort Ord.

I am sure it was the Lord's guidance that kept my mother together.

We lived in a little house on Munras street, rented from a farmer who owned the house in front of us. I 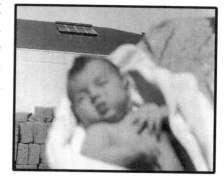 remember Mother being very sick. We didn't have a washing machine and dryer so Mother had to do the laundry in the bathtub with a wash board and hang the clothes on the clothesline. One day the farmer that owned our house drove right through Mom's clothes hanging on the clothesline and dirtied them with his muddy truck. She was so mad she cried for hours. I remember feeling so helpless and wondering how anyone could be so mean.

A lot was going on that children don't know about but later I learned that my mother was pregnant. She had been trying to have a second child for quite some time. She was finally pregnant, but was also very ill. She was told that a tumor was growing with the baby and it might starve out and deform the fetus. The doctors suggested she terminate the pregnancy. Mom refused. She had a lot of worries and hard days, and was so thankful that an older couple next door was always available to babysit.

Sharon's welcoming committee.
Mable Saunders (our Grandmother)
Mother and me

My sister Sharon was born February 9, 1947, a completely healthy baby girl. The tumor was gone. My mother was delighted.

The summer before Sharon was born, my dad's younger brother Frank came and stayed with us for the summer before his senior year in high school, and worked with dad in the plumbing business. He was only twelve years older than I and I adored him. He went back to Colorado to finish high school and after graduating he came to live with us while he got his plumber's training.

Frank joined the Navy in 1950 and in 1954 married my Aunt Jacque. They moved nearby in Monterey where they had their first two children. I adored my Uncle Frank. He was like an older brother and gave me the attention I needed after my sister was born. He was my advocate.

Not everyone was so helpful. The situation with the older couple next door, on whom my mother depended for babysitting, turned out to be a sad turn of events. The man was a pedophile and sexually abused me. When I told my mother what had happened, she was horrified; it was one more thing for her to deal with. I was never included in any of the discussions about the incident so all I know is we moved very quickly. It never occurred to me that I shouldn't tell. I was never threatened. In those days that kind of abuse was kept quiet. I am assuming it was a "she said/he said" situation. I think my parents were embarrassed.

Still, we needed a new place to live. My father worked with a man named Mr. Ogletree and he and his family were good friends of my parents. They let my parents know that a house had become available behind them on Cass Street in Monterey. We moved into the little house behind the Ogletree family.

The five of us on Easter Sunday. All dressed up and ready for church.
Kenny, me, Karen, Sharon and Gary

The Ogletrees had three children: Kenny was a year older than I was and Karen a year younger. The youngest Ogletree child, Gary, was 2 ½ years younger than my sister Sharon. We made a tight little group.

The five of us went everywhere together. We played outside all the time. We built tree forts, we roller skated, rode bicycles, played tetherball, and had a nice swing set. The empty lot next door was perfect place for us to play cowboys and Indians.

We walked to the Saturday

movies and we all went to Sunday school together. Our lives were full of fun with picnics in Big Sur, camping in Arroyo Seco and swimming in the river. Every Memorial Day we went to Yosemite for the holiday.

We didn't have cell phones. As a matter of fact we had party lines. The phone would ring and depending on how many times it rang you would know if it was for you or one of the other four families you shared the line with. We also enjoyed drive-in movies. We went in our pajamas because most of the time we fell asleep before the movie ended. As for a television I can only remember the *Howdy Doody Show*. We lived in a one-bedroom house and never felt cramped.

When I was about 11 my dad went to Alaska to help build the pipeline and made good money. When he came home he bought property up on the hill above Monterey, and started building a house. It was finished by the time I was fourteen. We all participated in the process. I got to learn how to paint, how to scrape the paint off the windows and general cleanup. Mr. Ogletree also went to Alaska and the Ogletrees built a house three doors down from us and our water skiing and camping trips always included them. For me, life was a family affair. We never had babysitters, and we always accompanied our parents wherever they went.

Dad built a boat in our garage and we spent every weekend either fishing or water skiing. My parents were fun and seemed to know how to keep us out of trouble and off the streets.

We had some fantastic vacations water skiing in lakes all over the middle part of the state. We also skied in the ocean and went over ski jumps and did some trick skiing. I was involved in ski racing and that took us all over Northern California.

My dad taught himself how to play the guitar, and one of my fondest memories was listening to him play. We would all sing together either at home or on our road trips. I remember so many of the old songs of the 40's. My favorites were "Roll Out The Barrel" and "Cruising Down The River." It was truly a family sing-along.

My parents were hard working middle-class people. They loved their children and each other.

My dad worked as a plumber and mom worked part-time cleaning motel rooms nearby. They were building their house and their savings.

When I was in junior high school, mom read an article about becoming a police woman. It was the first time the position was offered to women and she started studying for the exams she would have to take. She passed all the psychological and written exams and became the first police woman in Monterey.

In the beginning of her career she was not well accepted. The men of the community did not like being ticketed by a woman. One of her nick

May. Feb. 1114   MONTEREY, CALIFORNIA, FRIDAY, JANUARY 4, 1957.

Faye Saunders
Monterey's First Lady Officer

Badge 22 of the Monterey Police Department is worn by Faye Saunders. Five-foot-six with grey-blue eyes and long brown hair, she is the city's first lady parking meter reader.

This is the third day she had done her beat aboard a three-wheeled motorcycle. Until last month she had never ridden a motorcycle before.

Mrs. Saunders was appointed policewoman after a competitive examination. She has never been a police officer before.

Married to Willard Saunders, a plumber, she is the mother of two children, Carol, 14, and Sharon, 9. The family lives at 165 Via Gayuba, Monterey.

"I like the outdoors and hope to do a good job," she said. "I like associating with people. I am not here for the pleasure of writing tickets but since they are necessary I hope to issue them in a manner which will promote good public relations."

Last year $48,481.31 were deposited in Monterey's parking meters.

Born in Dalhart, Texas, Mrs. Saunders moved to Colorado Springs before she was a year old. She was educated in Denver schools.

Actually, she started work Dec. 1. The first month was spent in the offices of the department, where she familiarized herself with police routine, traffic laws and learned how to ride a motorcycle.

On her first day she issued 50 tickets, one of which was to a neighbor.

(Herald photo)

Faye Saunders, Badge 22 on the Monterey Police Force.

names was "Dickless Tracy". She took it all in stride and handed out the tickets with a" have a nice day" and a warm smile. After the first year, she was well accepted and respected. She worked for the Monterey Police Department for 10 years.

It was a little difficult for me as the kids in school teased me about my mom being a cop but I was proud of her for breaking the barrier, with class.

My dad was also a great shot and took great pleasure in Trap and Skeet shooting. He competed in many events throughout the state and won lots of prizes.

My parents were not afraid to try something new. They were comfortable with who they were.

They were competitive and loved an adventure. They demonstrated how good work ethics can make you successful. There was no laziness tolerated in our household.

Bend's Lou Saunders (right), a won a shootoff Sunday against Mike Redmond and Lee Smith of Chemult. hit 49 of 50 clay birds in the shootoff. member of the Redmond Trap Club, Grossmiller of Bend, Larry Sale of The four shot 99s, and then Saunders (Bulletin photo by Bill Ferrin).

50 YEARS AGO
Sept. 30, 1924

The Boys' Club of Carmel has presented the fire department with its first gas mask. For some time, Carmel fire lads have been agitating for gas masks to use in fighting fires.

40 YEARS AGO
Sept. 30, 1934

The old faithful "Daisy" arrived in the harbor today to drop several tons of cargo for local delivery. She is the only vessel beside the Nelson "Cricket" which has been in for the last week. The "Nayo" is due tomorrow.

30 YEARS AGO
Sept. 30, 1944

Lovely, small modern Carmel home for sale, completely furnished including electric refrigerator. Paradise Park section. Entire interior freshly repainted. $5,850 cash or terms.

20 YEARS AGO
Sept. 30, 1954

Some 8,400 acres of land at Fort Ord and the Presidio of Monterey is being offered for sheep grazing on a three-to-five-year lease, the Army announced today.

10 YEARS AGO
Sept. 30, 1964

Monterey Policewoman Faye Saunders won first place for women in the statewide pistol shooting competition for law enforcement agencies Sunday in Tracy.

Monterey Peninsula Herald —
30 Sept 1974

HE BULLETIN 13
nd, Ore., Tuesday, April 10, 1973

Redmond shooters win again

The Redmond Trap Club apparently wants permanent possession of the trophy awarded annually to the winner of the "Championship Shootoff" segment of The Bulletin Telegraphic Trapshoot.

The Redmond shooters won the title Sunday for the third straight year, recording a five-shooter total of 494 at the Bend Trap Club.

The Redmond team was led by Lou Saunders, Bob Ordway and Larry Sale—all of whom shot 99s. Jim Sharp hit 98 of 100 birds, and 97s were turned in by Glen Duncan, Harold George and Dwight Cork.

Saunders also won "Hi-Gun" honors. Seven shooters shot 99s, but Saunders won a 50-bird shootoff, hitting 49. George also won individual honors, winning the junior division.

Other winners were:

High woman—Helen Watkins of Wasco, 97; Sub-junior—Mark Bramen of Madras, 89; Handicap Hi-Gun—Lynn Engstrom of Pine Grove, 50.

Chapter 3
Married With Children

When I got older and started dating I figured out that if I didn't cook dinner, I would have to wait until we were all finished eating and then do the dishes. If I cooked dinner, my mother did the dishes, and allowed me to go out earlier. Win/Win situation.

One of the boys I dated was my first real love, Dempsey. I met him when I was 14 and my parents allowed him to accompany us on a lot of our ski trips. Life was good.

By the time I turned 15 my parents were concerned that Dempsey and I were getting a little too close and asked him, behind my back, to cool it down and stay away for a while. I had no idea what was going on but Dempsey did not speak to me for the next three years. He was hurt that my parents didn't trust him. I remember being heart-broken with no idea what I had done wrong. My parents could not stand to see me crying all the time so they eventually confessed to what they had done.

My attitude about life changed quite a bit and I retreated. I guess I just didn't want to get hurt again. I got a job after school and kept busy with just a couple of friends. I dated a few times but could never get past the love I was still longing for. I spent a lot of time praying that someday I would marry that man. Be careful what you pray for. God must have been very tired of my pleading for this boy from my past.

Just after graduation we happened to meet up one day and he asked me out. I was so excited I could hardly stand it. We dated for a while and then we married when I was 18 and he was 21. I had just finished Beauty College and he was an assistant dental technician. We were the original yuppies.

By the time I was 22 we had bought our second house, I owned my own business and was expecting my second child, having miscarried my first baby. I had been very nervous until I reached a certain stage of the pregnancy. Michelle Elaine Billey, was born January 4, 1965. I was so blessed to find out she was healthy. I never knew what real love was until I held her in my arms.

Michelle was such a good baby. She came two weeks late, and I always said we had a head start on her sleeping through the night. From the start, she was curious, honest, smart, and was potty trained before the age of two. Michelle wanted to grow up quickly, and was curious about how things worked. She was loyal to those who loved her, and always wanted everyone to be happy

My husband had decided he wanted to work as a Deputy Sheriff so he was now working 4:00 p.m. to midnight and I was working days. We left Michelle with a babysitter. She was a love at all times, and a wonderful baby. I didn't understand at the time how fortunate we were to have such a peaceful child. Still, Dempsey and I had very little time together and our marriage was going downhill fast. I didn't know what to do to keep us together.

Michelle and me just before Denise was born.

I got pregnant with my next child in 1966. I sold my business to pay off our bills and put money aside to pay for the delivery of our baby. I had hoped to stay home with the children until they started school. My husband decided he didn't want to be a family man any longer. We had a trial separation. I was 6 months pregnant and he was playing around. Our second daughter, Denise, was born February 22, 1967, prematurely at 4lbs 13 oz.

He told me he didn't love me but maybe he would again someday. I didn't know what else to do so I filed for divorce. The decision was actually a relief. His schedule and mine were always conflicted. We had grown so far apart and nothing I did changed anything. Deep down inside I knew he didn't love me anymore; it was time to get my head out of the sand and move forward.

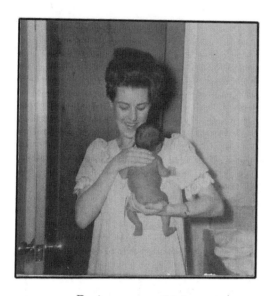

Denise was a small baby.

Now I had a very small baby that needed to be fed every three hours and a two year old to take care of. My sister came to live with me to help me out. She worked days but was available in the evenings. I felt guilty bringing a child into the world that would not have a father around. My mother assured me we would all be fine. I wish my prayer life had been active but I had totally forgotten all about God in the middle of all the trouble. I felt I was on my own and He couldn't possibly care about me and my troubles. How wrong I was.

Hindsight is definitely 20/20. By the time the divorce was final we had sold the assets, divided the furniture and gone our separate ways. I went back to work for the woman I sold my business to and many of my former clients stuck with me.

I bought a duplex with my half of the money and rented out the downstairs. My housing costs were small. I actually had more money on my own than I did when I was married. I was a saver, not a spender. I worked four days a week and spent the other three with my girls. I also had to deal with the fact that divorce in the 60's was frowned upon. I didn't discuss it with anyone. I felt judgment on many different levels, especially since children were involved.

I learned a lot about parenting. Denise taught me that I didn't know anything about raising children. She wasn't quite as easy to care for as

Michelle. In fact, her character was almost the opposite. She was determined to do things her own way. She was very active and into everything. She was what I would call a night person. We had a hard time getting her to bed at night and getting her awake in the morning. Later it was hard to potty train her because she was too busy to sit on the toilet. She was happy, full of energy, and daring, and she idolized Michelle.

Michelle and Denise's dad had two weekends a month visitation rights. This gave me the opportunity to go out at night with my friends.

My parents had also moved out of the area. They left because, as they put it, the traffic was getting too heavy and too many people were moving to Monterey. They were used to a quiet little town. Cannery Row was now a tourist attraction and the Bing Crosby golf tournament brought a lot of people to the area. In exploring places to live, Dad found Bend, Oregon. They bought a motel right on Highway 97 coming into town. Mom enjoyed meeting all the different people traveling through Bend. It was fun when we went to visit them. Mount Bachelor was a great snow skiing place and summers had fishing and a river that runs through town. We had our own room in the motel.

I had no intention of getting married again for quite some time. You lose friends as they choose sides and most of our friends had been with the Sheriff's Department, where Dempsey worked. I would get together with a couple of my divorced girlfriends and we would go out together. We had a pact to all come home together, no pickups. We liked to go to the Mission Ranch Inn, owned by Clint Eastwood and they had a singles night with sing along music.

One night at the Inn, I met a gentleman named Gill Goodman. Little did I know he would be my next husband. He was writing notes to some girl across the bar. I happened to see that his spelling was off and told him he had a great idea but he needed to work on his spelling. He decided that I was the one he needed. That was the last note he wrote.

We dated for about a year. He was in the Coast Guard and getting his Master's degree in Engineering at the Naval Postgraduate School in Monterey. I decided to take up golf since he was such an avid golfer. I was determined not to be a golf widow. It was the best decision I ever made. We played at the Navy course in Monterey and the Pacific Grove public course. It was on Coast Guard property with the light house on it. I really liked the game and the couple's tournaments we played in.

At the end of the year, we knew he would be graduating soon and would be transferred out of the area. We didn't have a lot of time to think about the next step. His criteria for his decision was simple: would his life be better with me or without me? He decided it would be better with me.

He made me laugh, he knew how to dance. There was quite a social group with the Coast Guard and great people that were committed to their job and each other. I was having fun for the first time in a long time and felt so relaxed.

Our lives were so different. He was highly educated, I was a high school graduate with a Cosmetology license. I had loving parents he had a family filled with drama. He didn't have any experience in fixing things and I thought all men knew how to fix anything.

I found this out the hard way. I told him if he wanted to see me he would have to come over and help me paint the interior of my new duplex. I was shocked as I inspected the bathroom he was assigned and he had painted the towel racks, had paint all over the floor and the walls were streaky. I never allowed him to paint any room again. One day it dawned on me that he would do a lousy job so I wouldn't ask for his help. I was a can-do girl and very self-sufficient. He wouldn't have it any other way.

A couple of days before the wedding.

26

Juke & Micki Goodman, Carol, Gill, Faye & Lou Saunders
Michelle in the middle

We were married June 16, 1968. He took on a wife and two little girls. He loved the girls. He thought they were funny. I would never have married anyone that didn't understand that my children came first and he had to care for them. We moved into Navy housing and I put my duplex up for sale. I was happy it sold for a profit, since I had owned such a short time.

Three months later I was pregnant with his first child. It ended up to be a tubal pregnancy that ruptured. This was a time when abortion was illegal and to terminate this pregnancy was equivalent to abortion. Standard procedure was to wait until the pain was really bad and then they would end the pregnancy. I was in a lot of pain but the doctor said unless I was bleeding badly or passed out there was nothing he could do for me.

Eventually the pain stopped. I called my original obstetrician and told him what was going on and he had me come to his office immediately. He was very concerned and admitted me to the Monterey Hospital right away. He told me that after the rupture, peritonitis had set in. I was a mess. He said I probably could not get pregnant again. That was alright with me. I was fortunate to have two beautiful daughters.

Six weeks later I got pregnant again. I was shocked and still healing from major surgery.

I was exhausted but carried the baby to full term. Debra Ann Goodman was born October 12, 1969. I was fortunate enough to have my mom fly down from Oregon to help me with the new baby.

Michelle, Denise and our new addition, Debra Ann

Debra was on time and a good baby, which was a good thing. When she was six weeks old, Gill graduated from the Naval Postgraduate School and we were told we were being transferred to Wild Wood, New Jersey. Prior to moving, Dempsey took me to court to set up a new visitation plan. He was awarded two months every summer. He would pay for their flights roundtrip. Michelle would be five and Denise three for their first flight back to California. They had to have escorts for the flights. I honestly thought he would get tired of the plan and stop sending for them. It never happened. He saw them every summer except when we were in Japan.

We went to Florida first to spend Christmas with Gill's parents, bought a car and then drove to Cape May, New Jersey. The three hour time change had us all out of sorts, especially with a new baby. While driving from Florida to Cape May, we would stop for our meals and I would ask the waitresses not to look or talk to Debra. Of course, they couldn't resist and as soon as they spoke to her she would start screaming and I would have to take her out to the car until she settled down. It was way too much for her to take in.

We found a motel in Cape May. When we woke up the next morning the ground was covered with snow. Gill had told me it hardly ever snowed because of the dampness of the area. All of us Californians had no winter wear and there were no stores open in Cape May. The Base Exchange had some clothes so we stocked up with whatever we could find.

We rented an apartment for a few months and now Debra was so far off schedule that we had play time in the middle of the night. I couldn't let her cry because she would wake up the downstairs neighbors. I was exhausted. It was a lot of traveling and changes and no family to help. Cape May was desolate, no cars, no people, no traffic lights—and *cold*. What had I gotten myself into? I felt like I was in the *Twilight Zone* and all alone. On the weekends I would go house hunting and finally I found a realtor that would show someone with a Jewish name like Goodman a house. That was a big awakening. I had never been discriminated against and was quite taken back that anyone would even ask such a thing.

I finally found a house in Cape May. We moved in and got settled. We met other Coast Guard families and I started to feel normal. The house needed a lot of work so I repainted the interior, had new carpet installed and then it felt like home.

The Coast Guard is a family all its own. We always stick together and help one another through the tough times. At Cape May it was truly a party group. What else was there to do? Party, spend time at the beach, and luncheons for the ladies with child care.

I have to admit I was quite naïve and would soon learn a lot of valuable lessons. The Coast Guard wives had many social functions and you felt like you had family and someone to talk to. We also helped one another, and this was all wonderful and welcomed. But I was not accustomed to gossip. I believed what anyone said, and I learned the hard way that anyone that would talk negatively about someone else would also talk about you behind your back. Since then I have become very selective in my friends and hold them to a high standard. If I feel like someone has hurt me or said something mean, I will go to a close friend to get their perspective. Often it has been the truth that has angered me and I have learned to deal with it and change how I think. Gossipers are usually that way because they need to make themselves look better than others.

I found out that I was pregnant again, and Jill Lynn, was born on April 1, 1971 and I now had four children under the age of 6. Fortunately Jill was on time and a good baby. With three older sisters tending to her every need, she had no reason to fuss. She was sweet and definitely a daddy's girl.

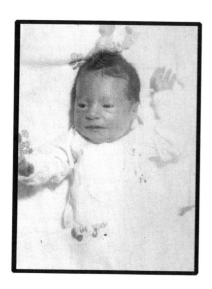

And yet, Cape May was difficult for me. I was busy 24/7 taking care of children, cleaning house, grocery shopping and fixing meals. This was not a time in American history that the men helped out, at least not in my family. My husband would tell me he worked for a living and home was my job. I had to learn to sew as there were no stores to buy clothes.

From Labor Day to Memorial Day the town essentially closed down. The local grocery store that stayed open had a limited supply of good meat and vegetables. There was a farm about 40 miles away and you could call and get fresh meat for the winter. I would call ahead and order by the pound each type of meat I wanted. They would package it for freezing and I would pack my kids in the car and drive to pick up my order.

From Memorial Day to Labor Day, however, the town was packed with people from Canada, New York and Philadelphia vacationing. Cape May and the nearby town of Wildwood were very hot and humid in the summer. We would spend our summers at a private military beach in Wildwood. We could cool down with the breeze off the water. All of us would meet at the beach and have cookouts and summer fun. We would haul the playpens and toys for the children to play with.

We always joked that you had to watch your kids because the mosquitos were so big they might carry one away. None of the ladies wore perfume, we wore OFF (a mosquito repellent), and we all smelled the same.

Michelle, Denise, Debra & Jill

These pictures were taken in Cape May in front of our house.

The picture on the left was taken to send to my mother. She had worked hard to find dresses that matched for all the girls. They were so cute and happy.

In June of 1973 we were transferred to Washington DC for our next duty station. I thought I had died and gone to heaven. The girls were a little older and there were so many things to do and see. We were gone all the time. We found a nice house in Clinton, Maryland and the girls could ride their bikes. The school was very good and within walking distance. We had a great neighborhood, with lots of children. In the winter we went ice skating. We visited the Kennedy Center, the Smithsonian Museum and many historical sites. I took my parents on a tour of the White House at Christmas time to see it all decorated. Shopping and entertainment was premium. The girls were thriving and happy. I could have lived in the D.C. area for the rest of my life.

CHAPTER 4
JAPAN

It turns out that staying in Washington D.C. wouldn't last. In 1976 my husband was asked if he would like to go to Japan and work on the LORAN (Long Range Aids to Navigation) stations in that area of the world. This was the way airplanes and ships could find out where they were and where they needed to go. He politely told them no before he even mentioned it to me. He knew that my mother was dying of cancer.

When he came home that night and told me he had declined that duty I was not happy. I should have been thrilled. After all, I loved where we lived and my mother had been fighting cancer for nearly a decade. But for some strange reason I felt we had to go to Japan so I told him to go back the next day and tell them we would love to go. Gill couldn't understand how I could leave the States with my mother being so ill, but as I explained, she was staying at the City of Hope hospital in California for treatment, three thousand miles away, so being in Japan wouldn't be that much of a difference. With four children at home and a continent of space between us, I couldn't easily leave everything and go stay with her. Besides, my sister Sharon lived on the same coast and mother was staying with her while she had treatment.

Gill left Washington, D.C. early to get things set up for us to follow him. I got the house sorted and ready to rent, cleaned and threw away stuff. We couldn't take everything with us as our weight was limited for overseas. The house we would be living in on Yokota Air Force base was furnished so we just needed our necessities. It was difficult enough figuring out what goes in storage and what would be shipped to Japan.

The other difficult part of going to Japan was having to get the vaccines to travel to another country. This was not a popular task with my girls. We were headed to get our shots and I told them that I would be first because I didn't want to watch everyone else get shots, I wanted mine over with fast. They must have been listening because when we got to the clinic and the doctor came out and asked who would be first, they all raised their hands and pleaded to be first. The doctor gave me a funny look and told me this had never happened before. I don't remember who was first but I was last. Reverse psychology paid off.

Gill came home to help us get our stuff together to fly to Japan. We decided to make a stop in Hawaii to visit some friends who were stationed there. It was four days of sightseeing. I had no idea we would live there one day.

We arrived in Japan in mid-August of 1976 and we were assigned to a four-bedroom house on Yokota Air Force base.

It was so exciting to be in a different country. The smells, architecture, streets, and landscaping were all so different. The roads were very narrow and everyone drove on the opposite side of the road. The houses were tiny by American standards and there seemed to be a small grocery store on each block. Every street looked alike and we could not read the signs. When we first arrived I told the girls we had a long drive from the airport to the base, so everyone needed to go to the restroom. When we got in the restroom, they were shocked to see that the toilet was a hole in the floor that you apparently had to squat over. When you are wearing slacks it is difficult to straddle the hole and squat. From that day on the girls always made sure they went to the bathroom at home so they would not have to use the public restrooms.

Being adventurous people, the girls and I were off and exploring as soon as we got settled. I had to learn how to drive on the opposite side of the road. It takes some getting used to. The children adjusted well to their new surroundings and we had many great road and train trips. I loved watching the girls playing on the playgrounds with all Japanese children. I marveled at how well they would somehow fit in and play with them. Language didn't seem to be a barrier.

The parks and landscaping were all perfect. The trees were trimmed and well taken care of. The gardens were spectacular and sometimes you felt like you were wandering through a bonsai world.

When we took our road trips I would have the girls count and write down how many stoplights we passed and which way we turned, right or left, so we could find our way back to the base. I tried not to drive too often. Taking the train was much easier. The trains were color-coded so if you took the blue train and stopped four times you knew to take the blue train home and count the stops backwards. All of the shopping malls were around the train station. You got out of the train, went upstairs and you were there.

One time, Michelle left her very expensive camera on the train. I talked to the train station person telling him we had left a camera on the train and he told us that the train would be coming back soon and the camera would be on it. We waited and sure enough the camera was right where Michelle left it. I later learned that in the Japanese belief system, anyone who cheated, took something that doesn't belong to them, or murdered someone would experience bad things in their next lives. I always felt safe in Japan. People were kind and appreciated the fact that I tried to speak Japanese. I took some classes but the language is very difficult. I could understand more than I could speak. The only time the Japanese were not nice was on the train during rush hour and at the airport getting their luggage. You could get pushed right out of the train at any given stop.

Another experience I had on the train reinforced my feeling of safety. I had escorted my mother-in-law back to Tokyo, after her visit, and now had to come back home. It was about 10:00 pm and I was reading my book when all of a sudden a strange man was swaying in front of me. I could tell he was drunk and I felt like he was going to sit down but there was no room. He made a lunge and I got up just in time. He sat down. I went to the door of the train and stood for the rest of the trip. The man started to get up and head my way, when suddenly two men stood in front of him and would not allow him to get up until I got off the train. They were protecting me and I was so relieved.

Early on during our stay in Japan I knew why it was so important for me to be there. Even though I was excited to be there I had a heavy heart knowing I would soon lose my mother. My friends' daughter in Maryland also had cancer and I was beginning to question if there was a God. I had grown up believing in God and went to Sunday school and youth groups and sang in the children's choir. But now things didn't make sense. How could a loving God allow all these devastating things to happen? I was searching for answers high and low, and behold God showed up just in time. I was invited to go to church with one of my neighbors. She was a delightful lady with such a heart for God and so loving. Her name was Dawn. Our children played together and we got along very well. I would question her and debate her on why God allowed such hurts and she would say she didn't have all the answers but she knew that God loved me and maybe I should ask him myself. She never preached, or judged, she just lived the life of a true Christian.

One night in church it was as if Jesus was sitting right next to me, beckoning me, to join him in this life's adventure. I accepted Jesus as my savior and have had quite a journey ever since. I gave all my problems to him and he has helped me through a multitude of adversities.

I had so much to learn and I totally gave him the reigns in my life. I had such a hunger to know more about God and attended every Bible study I could. It hasn't been easy because I was a very stubborn person, opinionated with quite a negative attitude. I felt that if anything could go wrong, it would, if it concerned me.

Feeling sorry for myself was high on my list. After all I had four children and a husband who was gone quite a bit, and I was overwhelmed at times with the responsibility. I thought I could do it all myself but after I met Jesus he has helped me overcome so many of my faults and attitudes even in the worst of times. I can honestly say that without my faith I would not have made it past the age of 40. I don't understand how anyone thinks they don't need any heavenly help. We think we are in control but we have no idea how little control we actually have. God gives us hope in all situations.

The first miracle I experienced happened around the time when I got a call that my mother had had a stroke in Bend, Oregon, and was not expected to live very long. I knew that I could get a flight through the military on an emergency leave. A friend was going to take care of my children, so I packed my bags and was off to the airport to check if there was any space available on flights going out that day. I was told the flight going out late that afternoon was full and there were no other flights that night. A still small voice told me to sit tight and wait.

I got my book, sat down and began to read. I had dinner at the airport and continued waiting, wondering if I had lost my mind. I was the only person left in the airport. The man at the counter told me once again that there were no more flights and I told him I understood.

Soon all the passengers who were supposed to leave on that earlier flight came back in and had to sit in the waiting room because they had already gone through customs and could not come back into the airport area. The airplane had mechanical problems and they had been sitting out on the tarmac for quite some time while I had a nice dinner and sat comfortably. The intercom came on and paged a Carol Goodman. I went up to the counter and was told that a new plane was assigned to fly in to McCord Air Force Base and there would be room on it for me. All reason had told me to go home and come back tomorrow, but God had a better plan. I was on my way knowing that God had made all the arrangements. When I got on the plane we were given a sack lunch and uncomfortable director-type seats. The flight would take nine hours and we were sitting backwards with a lot of equipment on the plane behind us. I was nervous but I went to sleep right away (thank you God) and arrived in what seemed like minutes.

When we arrived at McCord Air Force Base in the Tacoma area of Washington I was asked if I wanted a bus to Seattle or to the Portland airport. It seemed to me that Portland was closer to Bend, but again that still small voice said "Go to Seattle." Okay, I thought, maybe I was supposed to call my uncle in Seattle and let him know about his sister and meet him there. I find it very interesting how I rationalize why God would have me go in a different direction. I am always trying to second guess him. I must keep him amused.

When I got to the Seattle Airport I was told that the flight was full so I put my name on standby. For all I knew, someone had better plans for me. I called my uncle and told him about my mother and he said if I didn't get a flight out to call him and he would pick me up and drive me to Bend the next day. Again I was paged and told there was room for me on the plane and we would be leaving soon. As we were flying over Portland the pilot informed us that the Portland Airport had been closed for three days due to heavy fog conditions and bad weather. This was November. If I had chosen to go to Portland to catch a plane to Bend, Oregon, I would have been stuck at the airport for several days. The decision to go to Seattle gave me a direct flight to Bend. God always has a better plan.

Mom had been diagnosed with breast cancer in 1967. She had a full mastectomy and several lymph nodes removed. The doctors said she would be fine. She'd had no chemotherapy. Instead, she had Cobalt treatments, the substitution at that time for radiation. The doctors assured us that the cancer was gone and would never return. Two years later she learned she had a malignant tumor in her left lung and that was removed. Two years later she got cancer in both lungs and also needed a hysterectomy and an adrenalectomy. The doctors said taking away the hormones would slow down the spread of cancer. My sister got the doctors in Bend to release her and recommend her to the City of Hope in California and took care of her while she was going through treatment. She saw the daily turmoil mom was experiencing. The City of Hope's doctors were the experts in the field and their treatments gave her a little more time. The cancer was slowed down but then it went to her bones. From the bones the cancer went to the brain and caused a stroke. The doctors knew her time on this earth was coming to an end.

We had seen her briefly when we stopped on our way to Japan. At that time, she had lost three inches in height in six months and was miserable. She hurt all over but was very brave during our visit. The girls had no idea why Grandma was so quiet.

I was fortunate enough to spend two weeks with Mom before she passed away. I was able to say goodbye and keep her company before she left her earthly body for a heavenly one. I stayed for another week to help my dad sort out the paperwork and some of her things. He was now alone. I hugged him, tried to help him get settled, then headed back to my family in Japan.

When I returned, we had another problem waiting. We had not sold our house in Maryland, thinking we might be transferred back. However, we learned that the renters moved out and had left some fire damage in the kitchen. Our neighbors cleaned it up and called a realtor to sell it. We had payments to make on the vacant house and repair payments and we were strapped for money. While I was in church I clearly heard the Lord speaking to me,

"Put all the money in your wallet in the offering this morning".

I argued that I had very little money left and we were strapped.

He said "do it any-way"

I obeyed and to my amazement within days our house sold and we actually made money on it. I have learned that giving comes back to you by a bigger margin than you can ever imagine. Obedience to God is the key to success.

Japan had a big smog problem. Mount Fuji was so close but you could only see it when the Kanto winds blew the smog out to sea. This smog caused me to have two spontaneous lung collapses. The first time I had a 90% collapse. The second time, I knew what was happening so I got to the hospital sooner, and I "only" had a 25% collapse. Again, God was watching over me. The doctor said he wanted to send me to the Philippines or to Hawaii to a medical facility for lung surgery. I would have to stay away from my family for six weeks because you can't fly right after lung surgery. I told them no. Unless the lung condition was life threatening I was not interested. Again I called on God and gave him this problem to Him and I have never had another collapse. I firmly believe He prevented it from ever happening again.

We had built a community in Japan. I was happy there. I was involved in an exchange of customs with the Japanese women off-base. They learned our customs and we learned theirs. We gave the first baby shower to one of these women, and the Japanese women were so excited. They loved the cakes, pies and cookies we would bring to our sessions. Their desserts were quite bland. One fun memory was spraying one of the pies with whipped cream and immediately one of the ladies said,

"Eew! Shaving cream on the pie?"

We laughed and, after I coaxed them to take a taste, they were amazed and wanted to just eat the whipping cream.

We prepared a Thanksgiving meal for them and we experienced their Tea Ceremony. We took turns celebrating each other's holidays and would explain what they meant. For instance, the Japanese take off the entire first week of New Year. They prepare all  their food ahead so no one cooks during that time.

Summer rolled around and I told the ladies we had to suspend our time together because the children were out of school. They told me to bring the kids and meet them at the train station. They took the girls and me to some of the most incredible parks and flower gardens. I could never have found these places on my own.

I taught English at a private girls' school. Teaching English in the school was only a matter of talking. They could read and write it but they had a difficult time speaking it. They had books with pictures and I would read the book and they would follow along and repeat the sentence after me.

I was amazed to learn that the girls in the "private" school had jobs to do after the end of the day. They cleaned the room, erased the blackboards, emptied the waste baskets, closed the windows and swept the floor. Now tell me what "private" girl's school in the United States requires that kind of dedication. Their parents would be complaining that the schools were paid and therefore their children were only there to learn.

Many of the girls had lived outside of Japan with their fathers having jobs in the USA or England. When they heard about my lung collapse they wrote me a note saying, "We are sorry you have a sick lung." They were a lot of fun and wanted to speak English fluently.

Once I invited my class to come to our church for a Christmas celebration. Christmas is not a big holiday in Japan.

Gill & Carol 1977

They all came on the train and off we went to church. I fed them dinner after church and they all went back home.

The restaurant we attended literally brought in fireflies to make the gardens look magical at night. We were out admiring the beauty of the garden.

I was happy there. We were all enjoying the adventure and the new culture. My faith was growing, and I was learning to look for guidance in our lives.

And then our tour was cut short. Gill was promoted, and was told that he was now needed elsewhere. We moved to Hawaii.

Chapter 5
Hawaii

Before we actually moved to Hawaii, Gill and I took a short trip to see about housing first. I was so depressed. I absolutely did not want to go. I couldn't stop crying and didn't understand what was wrong with me. How could anyone not want to go to Hawaii? Eventually, I figured it was because we could not find affordable housing there and would have to live in government housing once again.

Government housing it was. We moved to a small house on Red Hill, in June, 1978. The house was cramped for the six of us and I could not figure out how we were going to fit all our furniture in such a tiny space. There was one real advantage, however: moving into the house on Red Hill gave me the opportunity to meet my very good friend Kathy. We hit it off right way and we remain close to this day. I call her the angel that God had placed in Hawaii just for me. I had no idea then what life-changing events lay in store for me there, and Kathy was just the person I needed to have by my side.

I contacted a realtor and looked for several weeks for a different house with no luck; everything we could afford was too small. I had all but given up hope when I got a strange phone call from a realtor I had never met before and she said she'd heard I was looking for a larger house. She had one that was coming on the market in Kailua due to divorce and the owner was about to go into foreclosure.

I immediately went to see it and it was more than I could ever imagine. It was a three-bedroom house with a two bedroom, one bath guest house, large family room and a 20x40 foot swimming pool. The house was located about five blocks from the beach. The kids could walk to school and there was a small triangle park at the end of the block where all the neighborhood kids gathered.

We were moved and settled in time for the girls to start school in Kailua. Life was good.

We spent time doing some painting, replacing carpet and general cleanup. The girls loved coming home from school and swimming. All their friends would come for a swim but most of the time they just enjoyed being together. Our neighborhood was filled with kids and they played outside on the street and at the park. I never worried about where they were. They were always with a crowd of good kids.

Once we were settled, Gill had told me it was time for me to go back to work. I couldn't imagine going to work. Besides what would I do? My hairdressing license was long gone and I had no secretarial skills or desire. I had not worked outside the home in so long that I just couldn't wrap my mind around it. I prayed and told God that if I was supposed to go back to work that someone would offer me a job. That felt safe. After all, who would offer me a job?

Gill and I were playing golf one day when a gentleman joined us. After playing a few holes the man asked me if I would like to come and work for his company. I almost fainted. I knew immediately that I had to say yes and I didn't even know what I would be expected to do. It didn't feel any better once he explained what his company did. He owned a tax preparation company called Aikane Tax Services and I would do income taxes for the citizens of Kailua. I wondered how on earth would I ever be able to do this.

He had sites all over Oahu located in the Bank of Hawaii because it was convenient for their customers. He explained that in early January he would start training me for the job and I would be able to do taxes that same year. I was skeptical. I am not even close to being a math person. I was very frustrated but with God's help I was ready to do taxes on time. I actually enjoyed the job and the people at the bank. I had banking hours so I was able to be home when the girls got home from school. I did not work on weekends and worked from January through April. Perfect!!! "THANK YOU LORD."

Then the bottom fell out of our world. We experienced a traumatic event no one should ever have to experience. I don't know how anyone survives without losing their mind and the will to live unless they know the love of our faithful God.

I had been worried about my eldest daughter, Michelle, who was now 15 years old. She didn't seem happy. Her boyfriend had joined the Navy and left for basic training in California. I had been told she was experimenting with marijuana. I was unsure about her choice of friends. She seemed unhappy and disconnected in Hawaii. She asked me if she could go live with her biological father in California and, after much thought, I told her if that was what she really wanted, I wouldn't stop her. I said many prayers for her safety and happiness. I had no idea what was coming. It was as if she knew she would not be with us much longer.

It all started with a beautiful day in Hawaii. Everyone had been busy and was looking forward to a quiet dinner at home. I was in the kitchen getting ready to cook dinner. Denise was talking on the phone.

Suddenly the operator broke into Denise's phone call and told her it was an emergency. She needed to speak to a Mrs. Goodman. Was she available?

Denise handed me the phone. The operator told me that Michelle had been in an automobile accident and that I should go to the local police station to find out what had happened. I honestly felt a little put out at being called away, assuming that Michelle had probably been in a fender bender. I was not worried. The town was so small, how could any accident be deadly? Just a bit earlier we had discussed the fact she had a final exam the next day in school and she was going to walk to her friends' house to get some notes. She said she'd be home soon.

Denise, for some reason, knew it was bad. She called her best friend and the friend and her mother came over to be with the girls. Gill was already on his way home from work. I instructed the girls to tell him where I would be and to stay home until I knew what had happened.

I drove to the local police station, irritated. None of this made any sense. When I got to the local police station the officer behind the desk informed me that the accident was serious but he didn't have any details. All he knew was that the accident involved Michelle. He said "one girl was dead and the other on the way to the hospital." He didn't know who it was and that I would have to go to the hospital to find out.

I walked to my car, in a state of shock and panic. How could this be happening? Why were they in a car? Neither girl had a driver's license. Gill drove up and I told him what I'd heard and that I had to go to the hospital to find out who was alive. I asked him to go home to take care of the girls and be there if anyone showed up with information regarding the accident.

It was about a five mile drive to the hospital, an unbelievably long way. What would be the fate of my daughter's life? I began to cry and ask God to help me. How would I live without her? Then I stopped.

"Lord how do I pray?" I can't pray for someone else's child to be dead but I don't think I can handle the news if it's Michelle. "Lord, how do I pray?"

And then I knew how to pray.

"Lord, if this cup can pass from me, please let it pass. But if it be your will, give me the strength to bear the loss. Oh Lord, how will I live without her? Please help me. In your Holy Name I pray. Amen!"

I said that prayer on January 31, 1980. I call it my visit to the Garden of Gethsemane.

I walked into the emergency room and asked for the name of the girl they had just brought in, the one who had survived the accident. They told me her name was Alice. My heart stopped beating and I could hardly breathe. Where was Michelle? She had just turned 15 and now she was gone. I asked if I could talk to the Alice.

"How could this happen?" I asked. "Whose car were you in and why?"

Alice was still in shock and was afraid to answer me. She said she was sorry and I left. The tears rolled down my eyes and my heart was broken. Would I ever be the same again? I knew my life had just changed forever.

Gill couldn't wait at home so he drove up just as I was walking out of the hospital entrance. I told him the horrible news. We both just sat on the bench outside in a state of shock wondering how our lives could change so dramatically without warning. We each drove home in our separate cars and knew we had to tell Michelle's sisters that she was no longer with us. I don't know how I got home, I was crying so hard. I had to calm down so I could face her sisters and tell them the news. When I walked into the house, they knew the moment they saw me. They started crying. Denise started throwing things and having a real meltdown. She was angry. There were many questions of how, why, where, and what do we do now. I had no real answers.

It was an evening of turmoil and confusion. God put his plan in action. He sent a young deacon named Paul from a church that Michelle's friends attended. Many of the kids had actually seen the accident and knew immediately that their friend was dead. Some of the kids ran to the church to seek counseling and advice on what they should do, and they told Paul about the accident. He asked who it was and where the family lived. He came to our house immediately and offered his services. He noticed that we had not had dinner, so he excused himself and said he would be right back. He came back and brought us a full turkey dinner with all of our favorite side dishes. Only God could have known what we liked.

We had bought the girls tickets to go see the Globetrotters and we insisted they go. They were not happy about leaving the house but Gill and I needed to discuss what we had to do. I had to call family and friends and I dreaded that. How could I ruin their lives? Plan a FUNERAL? No way! Parents are supposed to plan graduations and weddings. Trust me, there were no books on how to do all of this. I was overwhelmed.

I called my father, my sister and Michelle's biological father. I didn't want to give them this news. I knew their hearts would also be broken. They all came as soon as they could get a flight to Hawaii.

My other angel was Kathy. I called her right after we found out about the accident. "Hold on," she said, "I'll be right there." She showed up with her suitcase in hand and told me she was staying until my family arrived. She took all the phone calls, fed my children, and wrote down who brought food and flowers. She watched the girls as Gill and I set out to find a place to bury our daughter. We went to several places and then Gill remembered that he was qualified to be buried in a National Cemetery. He called the Punch Bowl Cemetery office and they told him he could give his spot to our daughter. The decision was made. She would be buried in Punch Bowl.

That first night I could not sleep so I got up, put my clothes on and started to go for a walk.

Kathy heard me and said, "Wait up. I'll walk with you." We walked for what seemed like hours. I wanted to see where the accident happened. I had been told it happened in Lanikai and that was not very far from our house.

We looked for signs of the accident but we never could find it. I guess God thought I wasn't ready to see the accident site. We walked the beach, and I threw rocks in the water. I was angry.

We watched the sun come up. I yelled at God telling him "I prayed for you to take care of her, not take her home." When I asked him why, all he told me was "When you see a parade, you see one float at a time. When I see a parade I see the beginning and the end all at once. It was her time." Kathy was around quite a bit, she kept me busy and listened to me. We took bonsai classes and Bible studies and attended prayer meetings. She didn't tell me "TIME WILL HEAL." She just listened, cared and prayed with me. She was my sounding board. What a friend.

I later learned that Alice had borrowed a car from where she was babysitting and picked up Michelle for a little joy ride. It was a Jaguar convertible. They had been showing off for a bunch of kids and when they went too fast around a curve, the car flipped upside down, landed on Michelle and killed her instantly. Alice was thrown free and suffered some broken bones and severe bruising.

It was time now to have a very serious talk with the girls. I had seen Michelle because I had to take clothes for her to be buried in. I saw her again a little later to approve how she looked. She did not look like a teenager; she looked matronly. In other words she did not look like she did a few days ago. The girls told me they wanted to see her. I didn't know why but they were adamant about it. I explained that she didn't look like herself and that maybe seeing her in the casket might be a memory that would haunt them. I told them that Michelle was in Heaven. Her spirit was with Jesus. They all decided, yes, they wanted to say goodbye.

I found out later that kids at school had said horrible things about Michelle's head falling off and how disfigured she was. The girls didn't trust me to say she was all in one piece; they had to see for themselves. Years later, I learned that at least one daughter wishes she had never seen her that way.

We had been going to a little Hawaiian church around the corner from our house for several months. They agreed to hold the service for us and sang the Aloha song. The church was packed with standing room only. I later learned that the little church normally did all their services in Hawaiian, but they spoke and sang in English when we attended. It was a beautiful service. I will always be grateful for the love they showed us.

Sometime later I drove to the where I thought the accident happened and it was very obvious where it had been. There was broken glass, litter and a fender on the side of the road. God protected me that first night. I was not to pay attention to where it happened but what was I going to do next.

About six weeks later I had decided it was time to take out the photo albums and look at all the pictures of my beautiful daughter. As I flipped through the pages, I started crying, I felt as though I was at the bottom of a pit and I might not make it back. How could I go on? It seemed too hard. Just then the doorbell rang. I didn't feel up to facing anyone, so I waited for the person to go away. The doorbell just kept ringing, so I finally answered. It was Paul. He told me he had a message for me. God told him there was a storm raging all around me and that I was not to let the storm get inside as it would destroy me. I knew immediately that God had heard my moaning and plea for help.

Paul was around most of that year. He asked me questions about how I was feeling and told me he needed to know these things as someday he would have to offer help to someone in his parish and he wanted to know how best to serve them. It was also a great way of counseling without me even realizing it.

I always called him one of God's angels. He was an obedient man of God and a very caring person.

Without my faith in the Lord, there is no way I could have ever survived such a loss without bitterness. I had many conversations with the young girl driving the car. She was abandoned by all her friends and had to change schools. She had made a terrible, life-altering mistake but she certainly did not want to see her friend die. I forgave her immediately and went to court to plead for leniency. I witnessed many miracles and physically felt God holding me up and I hold on to the scripture that "all things work together for good to those who love God and are called according to his purpose." Romans 8:28.

I remember complaining to God that I was not happy with only 15 years with my daughter. What a waste. He replied. "Would you have been better off never having known her at all?" My immediate answer was no. I learned so much from her and I would always cherish her memory. She was such a help with the other children and she had such a good heart. I loved every minute of her life. I just wanted more.

CHAPTER 6
AFTERMATH

One of the members of the parish that Paul attended designed a card for me to send out to all the people I wanted to thank.

*I am standing on the seashore
A little boat spreads her white sails
and heads for the blue sea. I stand and watch
until she appears to be but a speck of white cloud
where sea and sky merge.
Someone says, "There! She's Gone!" Gone where?
Gone from my sight, that is all. She is just as
large in mast and hull and spar as she was
when she left my side, and she bears her load
of living weight to her destined port.*

Around the same time I came across an article that fit my circumstances perfectly called "Stand Outside. Face the Storm. Have your Own Ben Franklin Moment." I have no idea where this came from but I know God always provides encouragement.

"It was during these storms of guaranteed destruction, God granted me impossible victory. Even though I don't believe I must go through a storm in order to see God's power I do appreciate it more when his power flashes against the backdrop of a terrible tempest.

"For you know that when your faith is tested, your endurance has a chance to grow." James 1:3 (NLT)

As hard as it is to accept, the destructive gale of an angry storm blows in an opportunity that comes to me through no other way. Because it is only after God erupts on the scene during the most violent of storms can I understand the joy James described—the joy of knowing God more.

When times are good, I know God loves me. But when times are bad, I have the occasion to see his love in action. After my dreams have been shattered, my course has been altered, and life doesn't turn out the way I thought it would, God's love is there to help me rebuild. Only this time I'm better for having weathered the storm. The part of me that has survived is now seasoned by experience. My new course is plotted more out of who I am becoming rather than where I think I should be going. I'm ready for the next storm.

How about you? Can you feel the headwinds of an approaching storm rushing past your face? Are life's darkest clouds massing on your horizon and pointed straight at you? If so, keep your faith. God hasn't left you. This storm is nothing to be feared. Rather it is your opportunity to grow and mature in Christ. Expect to experience the most brilliant and powerful lightning bolt of your life." Stand outside. Face the storm. Have your own Ben Franklin moment.

At the time of Michelle's death, Denise was 12, Debra was 10, and Jill was 8. It seemed to me that the two youngest girls took the news very well. They seemed distant, as though it did not concern them. Denise took it the hardest. Michelle was her biological sister. They traveled to their dad's house together every summer. Michelle helped Denise with school and friendships. Denise looked up to her big sister and now she was gone. She felt such a loss and said she did not want to be the oldest child. How could Michelle leave her? Denise became quite a handful.

It the midst of all the happenings, I did the best I could. Looking back, however, I realize that all my thoughts were wrong. My children needed support and help in understanding what this would mean for the rest of our lives. They should have had counseling so they could express their fears and anxieties. They didn't want to talk to me about it because they didn't want me to cry. I found all this out years later as they became adults and could express their feelings and understand a little better how keeping all this to themselves actually was unhealthy for them and their relationships. It made me sad to think that when they needed me the most I was emotionally not there for them. I was told I became emotionally withdrawn. I do remember saying to myself that I would never hurt like this again and I went about doing my job but not being emotional about many things. I asked my daughter her perspective years later and she told me that also she didn't want to hurt my feelings. She felt she had not had not only lost her sister, she'd lost her mother too.

While I was mourning the loss of my daughter, my sister Sharon also struggled. She was helping Jon, her eldest son, who had been diagnosed with non-Hodgkin's lymphoma at age 9. Sharon spent weeks, days and many hours at Children's Hospital in Southern California. I would travel to see them a couple times a year just to give her a break. Jon was sent home to die and my dad picked him up and brought him to Hawaii. I had our prayer group praying over him and for him and we asked for his healing.

While he was with me, my sister got quite sick, and was stationed on the toilet with severe diarrhea. It was the only way God could get her to sit still long enough to read a book that someone had dropped off for her. The book was *"How I Conquered Cancer Naturally"*. When Jon came home from Hawaii, he and Sharon headed off to Boston to the Hippocrates Health Institute to hear all that she could do to help Jon recover from cancer and all the damage from chemotherapy and radiation. It was a long process. She worked very hard to keep him alive and within five months he was back in school and recovering. My sister did a lot of juicing so he could get as many nutrients in a drink as possible. Juiced wheat grass was a major healing source for him. Our diets are important to our health. He lived and is now in his 40's and married. God is good.

The process Jon went through to get healthy again, after cancer, changed all our lives. We changed our eating habits dramatically. We ate more fresh fruits and vegetables and cut out white bread and as much sugar as we could. We also limited the amount of meat and processed food in our diet. It was hard on the girls at first, but they finally reached a point where they enjoyed the new diet.

Through all of this worry over Jon, my grief over Michelle's death was never far from my mind. One day, about a month after the accident, an attorney showed up at our door and left his card in case we wanted to file a law suit. Gill wanted me to meet with him and used the excuse that he was a Christian lawyer. I told my husband that I did not want to be the cause of another family's stress. It was an accident. Still he convinced me to go and talk with the attorney anyway just to hear what he had to say. At the end of the attorney's explanation of how much money we could receive I told him there was only one way I would ever sue. He looked encouraged, dollar signs in his eyes. I told him that I would only sue if it would bring my daughter back. He said "I'm sorry I can't make that happen". That was the end of any discussion about suing.

I was reminded by God to do unto others as you would have them do unto you. What if the driver of that car had been my daughter? How would I want to be treated? Forgiven or treated harshly?

Years later, after the availability of the Internet and email, I reached out to a few of the girls who were Michelle's friends. It was helpful for my own healing. Most had grown up and moved away, married and had children. They had gone on with their lives, but not without heartache.

I learned from Kathleen, one of Michelle's closest friends, that she had tried to prevent the accident. She wrote:

My parents both died of cancer and are buried at Punch Bowl. I used to go there and see them and then up to Michelle's grave to put flowers. The accident changed my life by making me realize just how quickly you can lose someone you love. Also I stopped drinking and smoking cigarettes. I switched schools too....I was a mess after I heard that she was gone. I don't know if you remember but I called your house that afternoon to try and stop Michelle from going. Alice had wanted me to go and I told her she was crazy. I told my mom when I got home and then I called your house. I think Denise answered and told me that Michelle had already left, but wasn't with Alice. I just wish I had run home from the bus stop because maybe I could have stopped her. All these years I have blamed myself.

I also heard from Alice herself. She had gone to college in California, and moved to Maui where she lived on the same property with her parents. Alice had been married for 10 years to a man named Paul, had a son, and was pregnant with a daughter. She had a full life, and a loving family. But, as she said,

I've had some difficult times in the last 20 years, but feel very blessed for what I have and am always thankful to those in my life that gave me the benefit of the doubt and provided me with more chances than I probably deserved. It hasn't always been easy...I've always been the hardest on myself...but having the faith that I have now has helped me in so many ways. ...There isn't a day that goes by when I don't think of Michelle...in some way or another. I talk to her ALL the time, mainly at night when the stars are out. She has, and always will be, my guardian angel.

The full emails are attached in Appendix A.

In memory of Michelle Elaine Billey

CHAPTER 7
PICKING UP THE PIECES

Just when we thought we were coming out of such a troubled time, the next storm hit and again I was not prepared for such a blow. My father died suddenly of a heart attack at the age of 59. It was 18 months after the loss of Michelle. Again I headed for Bend, Oregon to take care of planning another funeral. My father was the first of seven siblings in his family to die, and a crowd of relatives showed up. I was numb. I felt so alone and all I know is God got me through all of it.

My dad's siblings at his funeral, 1981. He was the first one to pass away. Back row, from left: Judy, Helen, Me, Bud, Mildred, Gladys (Bud's wife) Wilma, Frank, Jacque (Frank's Wife) Gill. Front row from left: Sharon Mildred's daughter and grandkids.

It took me over a year to settle the estate. By then I was actually angry. How could my dad leave me??? Why didn't I know he was having trouble? God had pressed it on my heart to go visit him just the month before but Gill and I decided we just couldn't afford the trip at this point. I was very sorry I didn't go and if I ever feel I should go, I will, no matter what. Maybe I would have seen or witnessed his condition and insisted he see a doctor. I have no idea if the outcome would have changed but I would have seen him and given him a big hug.

My marriage was a wreck. We hardly talked and Gill started drinking a lot and became verbally abusive. He was having a hard time dealing with this loss. He had no control over the situation and drinking was his outlet.

It has been reported that 75% of all marriages that lose a child will end up in divorce. The emotions are so high and raw and each person processes the event differently. The stages of grief are different for each person and Gill and I were not on the same page. He had no faith and no one to talk to. I asked the Lord for permission to divorce him and there was no doubt about his answer. It was a resounding NO!!! You can imagine all the turmoil in a family with everyone hurting in different ways.

It was a frightful time. I carried on my duties and tried to make life acceptable for my children. The Lord was holding me up but my children did not know they could call on Jesus to calm their anxieties. They had no one to hold them up, including me. I always reasoned that I didn't turn to alcohol or drugs and I took care of them, but they needed so much more from me and their father. They were afraid of what the future would bring.

It was time for a change. Gill got transferred and was assigned as CO of the Coast Guard base in San Pedro, California. We lived in Huntington Beach and again we were near the ocean.

I went to work for an interior landscaping company and I really enjoyed the job. The company would do the interior of hotels and businesses with shrubs, flowers and trees. After the installation I was assigned a route to go and care for the plants. I'd water and dust the plants once a week. I would replace any that weren't doing well. I traveled quite a distance in the L.A. area and thought it was quite interesting. My family life calmed down quite a bit. I had the weekends off and Gill and I played golf with a group of Coast Guard friends.

My Christian life was on hold for a while. I busied myself with as much as I could so I would not think about the past. I still had my faith but not my commitment. I did not attend church and thought I could control my own life. It always amazes me how we can see such miracles and then get too busy for God. This is not something I ever wanted to admit.

I would soon learn again, how little control I have. My eldest daughter, Denise, had been acting out her anger in so many ways and I didn't know what to do. She was running with a few kids that I really did not like. Denise broke all the rules without giving it a second thought.

My fear took over and I could not stand the thought of losing another daughter on my watch. She obviously didn't respect our rules. The lesson I learned is to get down on your knees and ask GOD what you should do. Pray for that child or problem you are having. His plans are much better than ours.

After much thought I decided to send her to her father's house in Santa Barbara, to live for a while to get away from the influence of her Huntington Beach friends. I felt a change of scenery would do her good. She had spent every summer with her dad so it was not like sending her to a stranger. Her dad drove down from Santa Barbara to get her. There was no big scene. I thought she would call to come home after a few weeks but much to my surprise and disappointment she never asked to come back home. Her new life seemed to suit her.

Years later she complained that I had abandoned her. I didn't call enough, I didn't write enough. I attended her high school graduation, sent money for college in San Diego, and visited her there. She came home for some of the holidays, and I attended her college graduation. I helped with her wedding and supported her in any way she asked. I thought I was doing the things that I should but it still wasn't enough.

Much later, I learned that she did not see things this way, and instead was deeply hurt. Denise and I have had a lot of deep discussions about the past and our history together. I have finally come to the understanding that she has frequently felt abandoned, and this has had an enormous impact on her. First, she never lived with her mother and father together as that marriage fell apart while I was pregnant with her. I think children of divorce have a hard time knowing where they belong. And, apart from two months every summer, her father was out of the picture most of her life. Then her father remarried and had a child, so she had a new half-sister. Then I remarried and gave her two more half-sisters. I'm sure that in her heart she was asking, "Where do I belong?" Then, her biological sister died and left her to take over as the oldest child. She lost her sister, her idol, her traveling companion, and the only person who really shared the same experiences with her. And then, from her perspective, her mother sent her off to live with her father out of fear that the road she travelled would only lead to disaster. She must have been asking her-self "where do I fit in?"

We lived in Huntington Beach for only two years. Our next duty station was Alameda but we lived in Novato, CA. It was government housing. I played bridge and bingo with the ladies group. We were only there for 18 months. Life seemed to be going well.

Debra, the next oldest, turned 16 and started driving a car. Debra respected our rules and if she was running late she would call. They knew I was a little uptight about driving and tried to be careful. They had firsthand knowledge of what could happen with careless driving. Debra was the only one in our family that has hit a deer. She didn't hurt the deer but it sure scared her. Debra had to leave her first boyfriend in Huntington Beach and she was missing him. Moving is difficult for young girls and we had moved plenty. I drove south a couple of times so she could see him while I visited my sister. The romance ended and soon she was enjoying friends at her local high school in Novato. She played soccer on the girls' team and was well adjusted.

Jill had a best friend that lived right next door. They spent a lot of time together. She had friends and seemed quite content. She seemed to be doing well in school. She was graduating from the 8th grade and was assigned to be the person in charge of calling all the students up to get their diplomas at graduation. I wasn't able to be there as I was traveling to Santa Barbara for Denise's high school graduation. Together we picked out a dress she would wear. Later, I learned, she had added a few extra accessories to her graduation dress that took on the hippie look. She told her father that I had helped her pick out the dress so he let it go. She is definitely an artist.

CHAPTER 8
MONTEREY

In 1985, Gill was offered a choice: He could take an early out of the Coast Guard or go to headquarters in Washington, D.C. He was not about to go back east so now we had to decide on where to retire. He suggested Bend, Oregon or Hawaii. I was not up for either of those choices so I told him I would return to Monterey. He was delighted so off we went to look for a house. I had been studying to get my realtors license and was looking forward to working in that field. While in Monterey we attended my 25th high school class reunion. We couldn't find a house on our first trip so we went back later and found a house that was just being finished. It was a lovely house with a green belt for a back yard.

We moved into our new house January, 1986. I passed my real estate exam to sell property. Although I worked at it for several years, I was never really very successful. I made enough to help with Debra's college tuition and have a little extra spending money. Yet if I figured out the hourly wage for the time I spent showing property, holding open houses and previewing property for sale, I made less than minimum wage. Obviously I was not very good in this field. I did better as an office manager and trainer for new agents.

Monterey is also the place where Gill and I became empty nesters.

Denise was already in college at San Diego State. She did well academically and thought about becoming a teacher. She had always been athletic and, when she wasn't working or attending classes, she spent time playing beach volleyball and soccer. We still had Debra and Jill at home, but they were both very busy. Debra was about to graduate from high school. She was very smart and had always been a good student. She actually liked doing homework. She was also an accomplished soccer player. However she found moving very difficult. She had attended three different high schools and the Monterey high school was so cliquish she didn't have any close girlfriends. She was ready to be done with high school. She moved south to study at the college in Santa Barbara, eventually graduating with a degree in economics. While still a student, she interned at the Goleta Water district, and after her graduation from SBSU, she went to work for the State of California Water District. She decided to get her MBA at Syracuse University's Maxwell School in New York, and later worked for several companies to help businesses with the planning process.

Jill was finding trouble wherever she could. Moving so many times makes it difficult for young girls to find a place to fit it. I also found that schools in each state or county are different in their curriculum. They were either way ahead of the students or, in Jill's case, way behind. It was difficult for her and she paid the price by not showing up as much as possible. But she was also very artistic, and amazed me at the things she was able to accomplish. She painted a picture of a horse that was fantastic. Her creative personality seemed to put her on a roller coaster of emotions. Whatever the emotions, she seemed to experience it doubly. When she was happy, she was extremely happy. When she was sad, she was extremely sad. When she was angry, well, watch out. She felt whatever happened in her life deeply, which was both her strength and her challenge. We finally put her in a continuation school and she did much better without all the distractions of the large classrooms. She graduated and went on to study cosmetology and become a hairdresser.

Gill and I filled much of our time playing golf. We started a golf tournament in Monterey and called it the Goodman Open. Many of our friends from all over would come for a great weekend of golf and fellowship. We always served salmon, fresh caught in Monterey Bay, artichokes, and baked potatoes. It was a tradition we enjoyed for twelve years.

A major family milestone was attending Denise's graduation from San Diego State in May of 1990 with a degree in communications. She stayed in San Diego working in sales for a large sporting goods manufacturer/distributor. She was really becoming more settled, and was dating a man named Bryan Finnerty who also graduated from San Diego State. Bryan was drafted to be a professional soccer player for the Detroit Rockers, in Michigan. We were excited for her marriage, and helped plan

Denise and Bryan were married September 21, 1991

and pay for her wedding. They were only going to stay for 5 years and that was about 25 years ago. Denise went on to graduate school in Michigan to become a teacher, and Bryan did well in business after his soccer career was over.

Gill and I were settled. The girls were growing up, moving out, and finding their own paths. But this time in my life was the beginning of a

major milestone for me. I became a grandmother. This was a time when I knew God had decided I needed to feel emotions again. For years I had unintentionally turned my emotions off so I would not ever hurt again like I did when Michelle died. That was a big mistake and I regret that my children lost their mom for a time. But then I got the gift of

Gabriella Michelle Santiago
November 19, 1992

Gabby.

Jill married early (the same year as her sister Denise) and gave birth to Gabriella Michelle Santiago on November 19, 1992.

I was so excited. It had been a long time since I held a baby in my arms. Gabby had lots of hair and a condition called colic. Jill was beside herself caring for a crying baby. I would call her and hear the tone of her voice and know it was time to take over. It was difficult not knowing how to make Gabby comfortable. We tried all the doctor's suggestions and some worked for a time but not long enough. When Gabby was three months old, she had surgery for a hernia. After the surgery she was the happiest baby and so much fun. I had decided that I was not going to be her caretaker so her mom had to find babysitters to care for her while she was working. I was able to see her at least once a week if not more.

I loved having her, and sometimes she would spend the night with me. Strangely, on these times she would fuss most of the night and I was frustrated not knowing how to help. When we took her to be tested for allergies, we learned she was highly allergic to cats. I had a cat named Mickey and that is why Gabby was so miserable at my house. I called my sister to come get the cat. I knew she had just lost her cat and would take good care of Mickey.

Eventually, though, I felt that it was time for a change. Denise and Bryan were in Michigan. Debra moved to Sacramento for a job. I loved being near Jill and Gabby and they kept me going, but otherwise, we didn't have many friends. Our social life was dead. We decided to sell the big house and buy a condo out on the Monterey Salinas Highway. I got a little more serious about golf and played with the women at Fort Ord. It was nice and it had a 10 hole, par three golf course, swimming pool and club house. It was good for practicing.

Gill had started telling me we needed to move from California as it was eating up our retirement funds. We argued about different places to go and could never seem to agree. I wasn't happy in the Monterey area but I had no idea where else I would want to live.

Chapter 9
Sequim

In August of 1993 we decided to take a trip north to visit DJ, a friend who had retired in a small town called Sequim, Washington. We started out toward Bend, Oregon to visit my parents' graves and see how the town had grown. We hardly recognized the place. We stopped by the motel my parents had owned, Bends's 97 Host Motel, which had been located outside of town on the west side. The town had grown so much, we had a difficult time finding the motel. We drove to Sequim and stayed with DJ for ten days. We toured the area, went drift fishing down the Hoe River, went to a salmon bake and played golf. The weather was beautiful and I fell in love with Sequim immediately. I knew we were supposed to move there. The Holy Spirit overwhelmed me that this is where I belonged. We bought a piece of property before we left town. DJ's brother-in-law was a contractor so we met with him to start the process of getting permits to build. Our lot was a little over an acre with a beautiful view of the mountains. I could hardly wait to move. Gill couldn't believe how easy it was for us (well, me) to decide right away to move. I was the one that said, "Let's buy a place to live while we are here." He almost fainted.

We went home and told our girls we were moving. Debra was settled in Sacramento and traveling a lot. Jill and her husband decided they would move with us. The plans were set in motion to move to Sequim. We started designing the house we wanted. We had enough money to build the foundation, and have a well installed. We would have to wait for our condo to sell to finish building the house.

We flew to Sequim several times to see how things were progressing. The foundation was in, the well was in and our condo was not selling. It was four years of going back and forth to check on the house and visiting our friend. The problem was that President Clinton had closed many military bases and several in Monterey had closed down. The market was overloaded with properties for sale.

I later realized the real reason we were not moving. In that four year period, Jill got divorced, moved to Baltimore, moved back to Monterey and fell in love with someone else. As soon as she told me she and Gabby would not be moving to Sequim with us, our condo sold. The escrow closed in two weeks with an all cash offer. The Lord knew that they should not move with us. It was time for him to work with Jill. I was always in the way by enabling her poor judgments.

In the process of traveling up to Sequim to check on the property we called Gill's sister and told her we were moving to a place she had probably never heard of: Sequim, Washington. She laughed and told us she had visited Sequim before. Her and Gill's Uncle Bill lived there, and she had gone to Sequim to attend the funeral of Bill's wife. Gill was shocked as he thought his Uncle Bill lived in Arizona.

When I heard that Gill had a family member in this small town I was very hesitant to move there. Gill's family was very different, disconnected and judgmental. We decided we would contact Uncle Bill on one of our trips and visit him.

Bill was a Godsend. I loved him dearly and we had a great relationship. He was a gentle man with a great since of humor. He was alone after the death of his wife, and I ended up being his advocate for medical appointments, driving him to places he needed to go and coaching him to move to an assisted living facility. I enjoyed his company at all times. He taught me so much. He was always so grateful for anything I did.

I remember driving him home after a visit to the emergency room and he had big tears running down his face. I asked him what was wrong.

"What would I have done without you moving here and taking care of me?" he asked.

"All I know is God must love you a lot for me to move all the way to Sequim to take of you." I told him.

He was a member of Sunland Golf and Country Club and he gave us his membership as he was 85 and not playing much golf. He challenged me to a match. I took him up on it and whoever lost would have to buy lunch. He always played from the ladies tees. I told him he was not a lady. Why would he play from the forward tees? He said being old entitled him to play from there.

We always joked around. There were so many great stories about Uncle Bill. He was the best thing that happened to us. Gill and I were reconnected to a family we didn't know much about. He and his wife never had children so we became his children with a lot of family time together. He had a stepdaughter from his wife but we never got to meet her. A couple of his grandchildren came to visit. He loved our children and would take us all out to dinner when they were in town or we would have a big family gathering and invite him to dinner.

One of my fondest memories was his last Christmas. We had gone south to visit our family for the holidays, and I went to see him when I came back. He had Christmas cards on the table he had never opened. I asked him why and he said he just didn't have the energy to get up and read them. I crawled up on the bed beside him with all the cards and opened each one and read it to him. As I read a card to him he would then tell me the story of how he knew that person, where they met and what they meant to him. It was a short history lesson of his life and

Uncle Bill's last Christmas

friends. He died in February and left me money from an insurance policy. I decided to use that money to take my sister and three daughters on an Alaskan Cruise in memory of Uncle Bill. Thank you Uncle Bill. He was 92 when he died in 2004. I still miss him.

Uncle Bill taught me how to grow old. My parents died before the age of sixty and I never got the opportunity to care for them or help them make life-changing decisions. I didn't know the changes that would take place with aging or the needs of the elderly. Uncle Bill was always appreciative and thankful for everything I did for him. He knew I had his best interests at heart. He listened to me when I made suggestions to make his life easier. He was not grumpy. I hope with all my heart that I will be as grateful and appreciative as he was. I will understand that any suggestions by my family to make a change will be only for my benefit and comfort. They are not trying to control me. Lord, help me to remember this.

I stayed active in other ways. Because of Uncle Bill's gift of his country club membership, we played a lot of golf. The first golf partner I met at SunLand Golf and Country Club was a gal named Marty. She introduced me to invitational golf tournaments. There was a time when I felt like I was on the professional tour. We had a lot of fun traveling and playing golf together. She also taught me how to make stained glass windows. She had been doing this for years and we would spend winters doing stained glass and summers playing golf. It was a great time.

Some of my stained glass projects

I spent a lot of time landscaping my acreage and tending the garden. I had found my home church and was delighted to have believing friends again. I still sit in the second row every Sunday and attend as many Bible studies as I can. I loved doing crafts and made many fun things. In my stained glass winters I made lamps, windows, terrariums and outside art.

We moved into our house in Sequim on July 1, 1997. Jill and Gabby arrived for a visit July 4th. Gabby was not happy we had moved and couldn't wait to see us. She stayed with us for another month as her mother had to get back to work. Gabby was four years old and a joy to be around. We went to the river and explored the many trails. We did crafts, read stories and had a great time.

We had to go back to California to get our boat and trailer to bring up to Sequim. Gabby got anxious to go home so off we went. On the way to California she and Grandpa had a disagreement about the noise her toy was making and she became very distraught. She cried out, "This is the worst day of my life and I wish I had never been born!" (We still tease her about that.) I pulled into a rest stop. We got out and I put her on my lap and explained that we could drive back to our house in Sequim and wait until her mother could take off work to come and get her, or we could be home the next day if she would listen to Grandpa. I promised her that when we stopped, I would make sure the motel had a swimming pool and she could swim for as long as she liked. She agreed and the rest of our trip was uneventful. She was glad to see her mom.

Gabby spent the next 12 years coming to Grandpa and Grandma's house for the summer. We had all kinds of adventures. Her mother would bring her up and then go back home to work. It was cheaper to fly her up to Sequim than pay for day care. When Gabby got older it wasn't about day care; she just loved spending time in Sequim with her grandparents. We have a great relationship because of all the time we spent together. She has only missed one summer coming up to visit and she is now in her twenties. She loved going fishing with us and is quite a fisherwoman to this day. She loved being my caddie when I played golf. All my friends loved her. We would play golf, she would take lessons and we always full filled our tradition of eating a Polish dog in the café after golf.

CHAPTER 10
GENERATIONS

I realized through Gabby that grandchildren opened my heart in a way nothing really had since Michelle's death. They allowed me to love and be attached again, but without the responsibility of being the parent. Over the next many years, I was given the gift of many more grandchildren. I always made it a point to be there when each grandchild was born. My mother had done that for me and I knew what a help that was. I could answer questions, do the cooking, change diapers and love on them. Oh the smell of a new baby and the joy they bring. Over the next few years, Jill and her husband Jerry gave us two more grandchildren. Sophia Marie Esquivel joined her big sister Gabby on October 15, 1998. Our first grandson was born January 2, 2000.

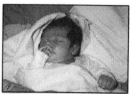

Sophia Marie Esquivel

Me, Gabby, Jill
Sophia & Joey

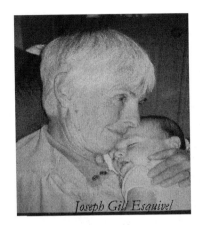

Joseph Gill Esquivel

The move to Sequim was great for all the grandchildren. We had so many adventures that would have never taken place had we lived in the same town. In Sequim we could go to the river, swim, raft down the river and have lunch. We had bicycles and we could ride anywhere we wanted. We went sightseeing to Hurricane ridge, the Dungeness Spit, Marymere Falls, Lake Crescent, The Game Farm and of course fishing in Sekiu. The parents also enjoyed the time spent at Grandma and Grandpa's house.

The other tradition was to ride our bikes to McDonalds for an ice cream sundae after dinner. I loved the visits with my family. We are an active group. Now they are all older and very busy with sports in the summer and jobs so I don't get to see them up here very often. We go south for Christmas because I can't stand a Christmas without children even if they are older. The grandchildren had fun and so did their parents. I miss their visits.

Sometimes I go to the river by myself and enjoy the sound of the rushing water. It is so relaxing.

On February 7th of 2000 Denise and Bryan's twins, Josh and Owen, were born.

I flew to Buffalo, NY, where Bryan had transferred to a new team, to help out and stayed for six weeks. She had some complications after the birth, and needed the extra time. The boys were real troopers being carted back and forth from the hospital to home, while mom was recovering.

Gabriella, Sophia, Joseph &
Jill at the river in Sequim

*Josh, Owen and Grandma at
the Dungeness River
and fishing in Sekiu*

Grandma surrounded by love, just one of the kids.

River rafting down the Elwha river

CHAPTER 11
BLESSINGS

The years passed quickly and Gill and I were feeling very settled in Sequim. But things rarely stay the same for long. Marty, my golf partner and stained glass teacher had taken a bad fall and shattered her shoulder. She never played golf again. I found a partner in a woman named Cheryl, and she and I hit it off. I joined her foursome on a regular basis.

In 2007 I was playing in a golf tournament with my friend and I wasn't feeling very good. I had a stomachache and told her to drive the golf cart slowly and stop hitting all the bumps. When I got home from the tournament, I went to the emergency room and was sent home with an appointment the next day for an ultrasound. Then I was sent to a gynecologist. It took six days before they decided to do exploratory surgery. I finally told them they had two choices. They could shoot me, and I highly recommended that, or they could go in and find out what was going on in there. I had surgery that afternoon. Much to everyone's surprise I had a ruptured appendix. Gill was shocked. He said when he had appendicitis he couldn't stand up, let alone walk. The doctor laughed and told him that was because he was a man. They don't deal with pain the same way women do.

I was in critical care for five 5 days, in the hospital for nine. The wound couldn't be stitched up because of all the bacteria. It had to heal from the inside out and cared for twice a day for the next two months. The wound developed an abscess and so it was opened up and cleaned and we were faced with another two months of daily care.

Again I knew the Lord was taking care of me. I learned that I was not in control of anything. I had to rely on others to care for me. I couldn't even shave my legs or bend over. I was not used to being so vulnerable. My husband did the nursing job with great care and my church provided meals and prayers. I heard God's voice: *Be still and know that I am GOD.*

Next the family came up to help and it was not about vacation. It was about helping me, and I was truly blessed with the comfort and care I received from so many. Living through a ruptured appendix is a miracle in itself. Many over the age of 50 never survive it. God was telling me it just wasn't my time yet. The surgery took place in June and by the end of October, I was playing golf again.

We went to California for Christmas and enjoyed family once again. Gill asked if I would be interested in going to Hawaii that winter. I hesitated because of the memories of Michelle's loss. I decided, however, that it might be good to get some sunshine and warm weather. We asked our golfing friends/partners if they would be interested in going with us and the plans were made and we left for Hawaii the end of January.

We stayed for two weeks. Gill didn't know all the options we had for places to rent on military property. We got a two bedroom duplex with one bathroom right on the beach. It was great fun even if we had to work the bathroom schedule to suit all four of us. Because of my previous problem I could not wait, so shaving and primping had to be stopped to let Carol into the bathroom. I must admit, it takes special friends to spend two weeks together with only one bathroom. We had great beach time and lots of golf. Warm and relaxing.

We made our trip up to Punchbowl Cemetery to put flowers on Michelle' grave.

I was glad we made the trip. I paid my respects and we went back to Hawaii every year for the next 7 years. We had much better accommodations on the rest of our stays.

On our 2008 trip to Hawaii we took on a

new task. We were scouting out places to have a wedding.

Debra, who had been working as a management consultant with the State of California, was engaged to a young man named Derek Burk. They decided they wanted a beach wedding in Hawaii. I needed to find the rules for weddings on the beach, a place for the reception and accommodations for the family. We went to a few restaurants and asked questions. We decided it should be kept simple, as not many would be able to fly to Hawaii for this wedding.

The wedding took place on Kailua Beach and the reception was in Honolulu at a restaurant right on the beach. It was a great time. Debra looked lovely and Derek looked quite handsome.

Derek's family

Debra's family

Debra had been told that she would probably never have any children due to some medical issues. She informed her husband that if he wanted children he was marrying the wrong girl.

Yet three months after the wedding she was shocked to learn that she was pregnant. Although she ended up losing that baby she now knew that she could get pregnant. She wanted a child.

A few months later she got pregnant again. She was so excited. On the next doctor's appointment she was told the baby didn't have a heart beat, and they would probably have to take it. They were going to wait until the next doctors appointment but things did not look good.

Gill and I were in Hawaii on our yearly trip when she called to tell me that she would not be having this baby. I was so disappointed and sad for her. I headed off down the beach and literally yelled at God.

"How could you allow her to get pregnant twice and then miscarry? It would have been better if she had never gotten pregnant!"

I was crying and angry. What was the point?

I stopped ranting long enough to notice the rock formations at the edge of the beach. There were many tide pools and I watched the baby fish, eels and crabs all swimming happily in the salty water.

All of a sudden the Lord spoke to my heart. He told me Debra would have this baby. It was alive.

"Okay I believe you," I whispered. "Thank you."

Later on I felt God telling me to call Debra and tell her the good news. I was very leery of doing this. What if I was wrong? What if it was my own wishful thinking? I would be putting myself in an uncomfortable position, and maybe getting Debra's hopes up. The Lord didn't care. He told me to call her anyway. I called her and no one answered so I left a message on her answering machine telling her that her baby was fine and would live. I told her to take care of herself and eat well.

She called back within an hour.

"Derek thinks you're crazy," she said.

I told her not to worry, he wasn't the first and certainly wouldn't be the last to think that. He said, "If we have this baby I will go to church every week for the rest of my life." I told him to be very careful what he promised because I would hold him to it.

Debra had a doctor's appoinment the next week and they heard a heart beat and the baby was growing.

Lola was born October 27, 2010. She was a very happy baby and very alert. It had been so long since I'd held a baby. Gabby, my eldest granddaughter moved in with Debra and Derek to help take care of Lola and go to college part-time. Gabby was so good with children and babies. It was a perfect arrangement.

Little did I know that I would be tossed from the miracle right into a trial. A few months after Lola was born I found out I had cancer.

CHAPTER 12
CANCER

Name: **GOODMAN, CAROL E** This copy for: Crim,Michael W MD
DOB: 08/20/42 SEX: F   Reg: 04/15/11
Medical Record #: H000128116 Submit D: Burghes,Erik M MD
Location: HRADPA Status: REG CLI Other Dr: Crim,Michael W MD
  Tumor Registry Reports Only
T ADDRESS: 71 WRIGHT RD   SEQUIM   WA   98382   Phone: (360) 683-5346

Specimen number: S11-1282 Date of Specimen: 04/15/11   FAX DATE: 04/25/11
  Received date: 04/15/11 FAX TIME: 0816

FINAL SURGICAL DIAGNOSIS

LEFT BREAST MASS, ULTRASOUND GUIDED CORE BIOPSY: INVASIVE CARCINOMA WITH THE FOLLOWING
FEATURES:

A. HISTOLOGIC TYPE: INVASIVE DUCTAL CARCINOMA WITH BASAL-LIKE FEATURES (SEE
    COMMENT).

B. HISTOLOGIC GRADE: POORLY DIFFERENTIATED.

    1. NUCLEAR GRADE: HIGH (SCORE 3).

    2. MITOTIC RATE: INTERMEDIATE (SCORE 2).

    3. TUBULE FORMATION: LOW (SCORE 3).

    4. COMPOSITE SCORE: 8 OF 9.

C. TWO OF TWO CORES ARE INVOLVED WITH CARCINOMA.

D. GREATEST LENGTH OF CARCINOMA IN A SINGLE CORE: 1.2 CM.

E. VASCULAR SPACE INVASION: NOT IDENTIFIED.

F. MAMMOGRAPHIC CORRELATION: POSITIVE (MASS).

G. INTRADUCTAL COMPONENT: NOT IDENTIFIED.

H. STATUS OF PROGNOSTIC INDICATORS:

    1. ER: ESSENTIALLY NEGATIVE, WITH FOCAL WEAK POSITIVITY (SUBOPTIMAL INTERNAL
        CONTROL - SEE COMMENT).

    2. PR: NEGATIVE (SUBOPTIMAL INTERNAL CONTROL - SEE COMMENT).

    3. HER-2/NEU: NEGATIVE FOR OVEREXPRESSION.

COMMENT: AS THE INTERNAL POSITIVE CONTROLS FOR ER AND PR STAINING ARE SUBOPTIMAL, REPEATED
STAINS ON THE EXCISIONAL SPECIMEN MAY WISH TO BE CONSIDERED FOR CONFIRMATION. HOWEVER, DUE
TO THE APPARENT TRIPLE NEGATIVE STATUS OF THE LESION AND THE HISTOLOGIC APPEARANCE, A CK5
STAIN WAS PERFORMED TO ASSESS FOR THE POSSIBILITY OF A BASAL-LIKE CARCINOMA. THIS
DEMONSTRATES DIFFUSE AND FAIRLY STRONG POSITIVITY IN THE LESIONAL CELLS, ARGUING IN FAVOR
OF A BASAL-LIKE CARCINOMA.

JZ/RF/jw

Olympia Medical Center Laboratory 939 Caroline St. Port Angeles, Wa 98362 417-7729

Our family has a history of breast cancer. My medical history continues that legacy. I write this accounting both to share what the experience was like for me, and to make sure my children and grandchildren are aware of their own history.

This story of my fight against cancer is taken from the diary I kept at the time.

On or about April 12, 2011 I discovered a lump in my left breast. The next morning I called my doctor and within two days I was set up with an appointment to get a mammogram, ultrasound and a biopsy, which were done the 15th of April. I was told the diagnosis would be back in about 48 hours but I didn't hear anything until the 28th of April—almost two weeks later—when Dr. Tatro, the surgeon, called and asked me to come in at 4:00 pm that afternoon.

Within an hour I got a call from my general practitioner, Dr. Crim, telling me he wanted to see me at 4:30. Sorry Dr. Crim, I am seeing the surgeon at 4:00 in Port Angeles. Dr. Crim told me to come in earlier, at 11:00 am that same day. Suddenly everyone wanted to see me at the same time. I knew something was up.

Dr. Crim gave me grim news: I had a very rare form of breast cancer, which was especially invasive. This type of cancer isn't responsive to most of the traditional treatments for breast cancer. It tends to be more aggressive than other types of breast cancer, is more likely to spread beyond the breast, and more likely to come back. The survival rates are also lower.

It all seemed so dramatic. Gill and I talked when I got home, and we both thought Dr. Crim was being a little over the top most of the time. His account was exaggerated at best. Later that day I went to see Dr. Tatro and her report was just as bad.

I told her that I had already planned a trip to California to see Debra's family and the new miracle baby. I was also going to my nephew's baby shower. I had already bought my tickets. We had a long discussion, and I told the doctor that I was going, unless it was a life and death situation. She gave me her blessing. The plan was for me to go to California and when I came back I would have an MRI in Seattle on the 16th, return home and make my appointment for the next day with Rena Zimmerman, the radiologist. She would look at my MRI and determine if I would need radiation before surgery.

In discussing my options she also decided I needed genetic testing.

Given my family history of cancer, insurance would pay for it. If the testing came back positive they would remove both breasts and do a hysterectomy. If it came back negative I would have only a lumpectomy or mastectomy depending on what they found while in surgery. We decided to postpone the surgery until we got the results of the genetic testing. I told them they had one shot. I would not go back into surgery at a later date when the test came back. It would take another two weeks.

For the first few days Gill and I walked around in complete disbelief. Neither one of us slept that first night. I had moments of great despair, disbelief and sadness and then moments of faith that I was in good hands and we could get through this. Faith was winning and my attitude was good, most of the time. Gill and I discussed what my needs would be during this process and came up with a plan. I would tell him what I needed and when I needed it. It was up to him to comply or ignore.

Off I went to California. My visit with Debra, Derek, Lola and Gabby was a real uplift. Babies and family do that for me. There is nothing like the sweet smell of a baby to take my mind off my troubles. On the second day of my visit I told Debra and Derek what I was facing and that all I needed from them was faith and lots of prayer.

Debra took it harder than I expected but I chalk it up to being a new mother and hormone-induced emotions. Not that she didn't care; I just expected her to be more stoic.

I waited to tell Gabby because she was in the middle of finals and she didn't need the distraction. I called Denise from Debra's house and she was matter of fact. Her dad was also dealing with cancer so she was used to the process and had faith that all would come out well. Her father was doing well so therefore, I would do well.

When I told Gabby, she cried and lamented that she knew several people that should have cancer and this was just not fair. She made me promise that I would do everything I could to get well because she was not ready to live without me in her life.

My next stop was Jill's house. Debra and Derek decided they would come to Jill's house too, since Jill had not met Lola yet and they wanted to be with her when she heard the news. I rented a car in Sacramento and drove to Salinas. When I arrived, Sophia didn't like my new ride. It was very small and bright red.

When I told Jill she took it much better than I anticipated. I didn't know that she had been warned that something big was up and she needed to prepare herself for bad news. She needed time to process this information. In the end she decided in her own mind that she would be a positive force in my life and do all she could to make life easier for me.

Despite the hard news, we had a great visit.

The next day Jill, Sophia and I headed to Irvine, California to attend a baby shower for my nephew Kurt and his new wife Michaela. My sister Sharon's family had endured a lot of pain and suffering with cancer themselves. Sharon had just had surgery for a cancer in her stomach and Jon had cancer as a little kid. He survived despite the doctors' prognosis of death. I had told my sister Sharon beforehand because I didn't want to ruin the shower experience for her.

The shower was very fun. Jill, Sophia and I spent the night in a really nice hotel, (free munchies and drinks for two hours each night and free breakfast). We only stayed one night. In my state of mind I could have cost them some serious money! We had dinner with my sister, and my two nephews, Jon & Kurt and their wives, Loraine and Michaela. They are a great group.

We drove back to Jill's house early the next morning. Jill got a little tired of my GPS recalculating. We made jokes about it all the way home.

On my trip back to Debra's house to catch the plane to Seattle, a song came on the radio that I had never heard before. The song was exactly what I needed to hear. The words were God telling me he would take care of me and lift me up. He would be there when I was in the bottom of the pit, and on and on it went. I was crying so hard I thought maybe I should pull over to the side of the road. It was the most beautiful, uplifting song I had ever heard. When I got home I went to a site on the computer to try and find the song. I don't know how many songs I listened to but none were the song on the radio. Many were similar but not the right one. I came to the conclusion that it really was God singing directly to me. It was his song and it gave me so much encouragement.

Gabby decided on her own that she would work out her schedule to fly back with me and care for me after my surgery. She made all the necessary plans and flew back several hours after me so she could complete her obligation with Debra. She went with me to the MRI office and drove home with me after it was finished. As things turned out the surgery was rescheduled so our time together was a great distraction, I could focus on something besides myself during the wait. She went line dancing with me several times, we rode bikes and she worked out with me at Sequim's Athletic Recreation Center. The Doctor had said I needed to do an hour of exercise each day to keep my stamina up. I thank all who rearranged their schedule for her visit. It meant a lot to me to have someone here to engage in conversation about life and futures, hers and mine.

The genetic testing (BRACCA) came back negative so now we could proceed to the next step, a mastectomy or a lumpectomy. That would be decided once they got in. Gabby attended the meeting with my oncologist and heard all the nasty things that would happen to me, including losing my hair, and it didn't sit well with her. It made her very sad. She also wanted to donate her hair to me for a wig but the cost was very high. I told her that it would probably be too warm in the summer for a wig and I would just wear a scarf.

During this time of waiting and travel, I was experiencing an out-of-body experience. The "other woman" had a problem, not me. Every time she tried to have a conversation with me about the future and how hard it might be, I shut her up. I did not want to hear from her. She had nothing good to say. It worked very well. I had control of what I wanted to hear or face.

When I told Debra about this other person she laughed and told me that was denial. I told her she could call her anything she wanted but I call her Rosemary and I didn't want her to interrupt my thinking at this time.

Rosemary and I came to together during surgery and I could no longer put her aside. We were in this together like it or not. (Rosemary still tries to get my attention now and again. She is not very encouraging so I still shut her up.)

Surgery was the 6th of June and it went well. Dr. Tatro removed the left breast and 12 lymph nodes. Two of the lymph nodes were malignant. I went home the next day and the drain tube was still inside and I was told how to measure the amount of fluids draining. My instructions said that after 48 hours I could remove the dressing. I thought the dressing was that 10 feet of elastic wrap around me, so I removed it. It was a bother anyway. When I went back to the doctor on the 13th of June and gave her my reports for the drainage, she informed me I was supposed to keep the wrap on to help the drain process. Now I had to wear it another 10 days and I really did not like the wrap. It was uncomfortable. It didn't do much better.

People were so amazed at how well I was doing. I got the drain tube taken out the 23rd of June and I realized that the entire area was numb. No wonder there wasn't any pain. As the area started to come to life again, it felt like needles, tingling. I am sure a lot of nerve endings were cut and they had to grow back. At least I was numb during the hard time, right after surgery.

I went to the oncologist to get my final orders and a blood test. I was set for chemotherapy on the 6th of July, one month after the surgery. The doctor explained to me that they give the anti- nausea shot first and then wait for it to take effect and then they give the chemotherapy drug, Adriamycin, with a syringe directly into the port they had placed into my chest. Then they add another drug, Cytoxan, in a drip that takes about 1.5 hours. I was supposed to put this numbing stuff on a tape they provide and put it on the port an hour before I show up so it will already be numb. The following day I would have to show up for a shot to get my bone marrow to start making new white blood cells.

I had a lot of time to think about this process. There was a short time I thought about not doing any chemotherapy or radiation. I could hope the surgery got it all and pray for healing and eat all the proper foods to get well. I decided that going that route jeopardized my recovery and I would do the chemotherapy and then get my body back to health. I was given a great book called *The Cancer Battle Plan*. I found it helpful and decided I will follow it as soon as the chemotherapy was over.

I also had time to do research on ways to help my body withstand the beating it was going to take. I found a product on the Internet called Miracle Berry, which was supposed to enhance my taste buds to be able to eat anything and take away the metallic taste in my mouth. The next product I found was a food-grade hydrogen peroxide to clean my fruits and vegetable, making them pure and germ-free so I wouldn't have to worry about the bacteria on these products. I was told that I might get mouth sores and this worried me, so I came up with a solution of chewing wheat grass at least once a day to help the healing process. Wheat grass is supposed to have great healing powers. I talked to my dentist to see if he had any great ways to protect my gums and mouth, and salt water rinses was about all he came up with. I told him I bought a juicer so I could at least drink good food and maybe even a straw would help keep my mouth from further damage. However he did tell me that fruit juices were not

---

good for these kinds of sores in the mouth. They could do damage to the gums and have teeth problems when this was all through. I didn't explore marijuana yet. It is supposed to increase the appetite so you eat and not lose too much weight. I decided I would cross that bridge when I came to it. I wasn't against it, I just didn't know if I would need it.

My golfing buddy and friend, Marsha, threw a dinner for our golf foursome on the Saturday night before my first treatment as a sendoff with good wishes for a quick recovery.

I had to shut Rosemary up because she wanted me to believe that all the side effects I read about were going to happen to me. I chose not to listen. I believed I was in good hands and those hands were better than "Allstate."

The dinner was wonderful; it was fun to be surrounded by my closest friends. We were gone a lot longer than expected. Jill, her husband Lon, and children, Sophia and Joey arrived that same night and waited up for us. They were there to support my first big trip to the oncologist. We chatted, hugged and went off to bed.

Sunday I went to church and Jill took Lon and the kids to the game farm and did some sightseeing. Lon had never been to Sequim before. Later that afternoon we went to the river on the bikes. The kids could not believe how high the river was. Riding bikes to the river and back was a good workout for me.

In the midst of all that was going on, Joey, my grandson, called me over and told me to close my eyes. I did as he asked and I could hear him rummaging around in something. He told me to open my eyes and when I did he had a wad of bills in his hand. I could see a $5 bill and several one-dollar bills. He told me they were for me. I was overwhelmed and told him I didn't need the money but he insisted I take it as he had much more at home.

"Grandma," he said, "that surgery must have cost you a lot of money and I want you to have this."

As the tears welled up in my eyes I told him that the insurance would take care of it and he could buy me an ice cream sundae at McDonalds that night. He agreed, but when we got ready to go to McDonalds that evening he asked me to hold the money for him while we rode the bicycles there. I took the money and put it in my pocket. Immediately he said, "There, now it's yours. Keep it." I tear up every time I think of how sweet that gesture was.

Early Monday morning Gill, Lon and Joey took off to go fishing in Sekiu. They fished when they got there and then spent the night to fish the next morning. They caught fish but none they could keep. They were disappointed. My friend Cheryl had been crabbing and brought us some wonderful crabs for dinner. What a feast.

We girls rented movies and watched movies all day. While we watched movies, Jill tied all my beautiful get-well cards to a ribbon to hang in my room. She couldn't believe how many cards I had. It took her quite a while. Wednesday, Lon had to go back home and I had an early (8:30 am) chemo appointment.

Jill and I tried to make excuses why we shouldn't go to chemo. We both claimed to be coming down with something but in the end we showed up. The first thing we did was go to the room to get the port set up. Then we went to the waiting room. Finally the doctor, was ready to see us. Again we tried to figure a way out of this but it wasn't working.

The doctor explained my odds and gave us some pointers on how to cope with this process.

The big tip was taking a double dose of Claritin before the shot, the day of the shot, and the day after. Although there is no medical science to back it up, the doctor said it would help with the pain of the bone marrow being forced to produce more white blood cells. I was told not to take antioxidants as a supplement during the time I was taking chemo.

The next process was to go into a private room, and sit in a chair. The nurse put on her haz-mat gear and got ready to start the chemo. They gave me five pills consisting of anti-nausea pills and steroids. The first injection of Adriamycin, nicknamed the red devil, was in a big syringe. She explained that she had to administer it very slowly as it could burn my veins. This is also the same drug that they tested my heart to see if I could take it. Jill set up our Gin game. The nurse told her that all her patients won when they played cards so Jill should just get her mind set on losing.

Next came the Cytoxan. It was a drip that was to take about an hour to get though the veins. When we were just about finished we told the nurse we were not ready to leave yet as we had ordered a pizza to be delivered. Just kidding! The look on her face was priceless.

The chemo finally finished, they sent me home. I felt drunk. As the Cytoxan was being administered I was getting higher and higher. They had told me the steroids would give me an abundance of energy, and make me want to redecorate the house or redo the yard. WRONG! I could care less about any of those things. At about 6:00 pm I got woozy and felt like lying down but I was afraid I would get the spins and throw up. I took one of the anti-nausea pills and within a few minutes I was feeling well again.

The next day I had to make another appearance for my bone marrow shot, which didn't take long at all. Thursday we had some nice chicken soup and I went to sleep easily with my drugs. Friday I had a headache. I thought the top of my head was going to blow off and the same for most of Saturday. Tylenol did keep it manageable, but I was told later that maybe it was a reaction to the Claritin so I knew not to take as much the next time.

Jill and the kids left on Friday night and Gill and I stopped at the Olive Garden for dinner on our way back from the airport. I had an artichoke and healthy green vegetable dip and he left me to order for him while he went to wash up. When the waiter came with Gill's food, we realized that I had pointed to the wrong item on the menu. He had to eat something he didn't even want. Chemo brain had already kicked in. That's the last time he left me on my own to order.

I kept a light schedule, visiting my golfing friends at a tournament, or joining them for dinner. I went to church and helped Cheryl with flower decorations for the Club. Many of my friends were surprised to see me out and about. I tired easily and had to take naps, but all in all I did pretty well. As I kept saying, God has my back.

The second treatment was on the 19th of July. This was Gill's first time to meet Dr. Nelley, the oncologist, and get the lowdown on the procedure. We played Gin and I beat him for the first time EVER. I had a few days of being absolutely exhausted and sleeping a lot

My hair was starting to fall but I was determined to hold on to it until after my golfing buddy, Mary Jo, and Alan's wedding on the 23rd. I made it to the wedding and reception but could not eat or stay very long. We brought home a doggie bag so Gill could have some dinner. I demonstrated to a couple of the ladies how easily chunks of hair could be pulled out.

They didn't appreciate my sense of humor. Marsha told me to "never do that again."

The next morning Cheryl came over to shave my head for me. It was quite a shock. I thought I looked like Dobby the house elf in the Harry Potter film. I realized I did not quite look like him because his ears are not pointed but just big, mine are pointed. I wore a cute hat to church and everyone knew why.

Jill arrived on the 26th of July we stayed busy running errands. She cooked up all sorts of things to fatten her mama up. I gained 5 pounds while she was there. I didn't quite make up the weight loss altogether but it was a good start. Pumpkin pie was our new weapon for weight gain.

She also went with me to get my new prosthesis. I was amazed at how many shapes of boobs there are. We were there for quite a while trying different bras and boobs. We also went to the wig shop and I bought a red wig, some small beanies and a scarf. Jill found lots of goodies to take back to her family. Cheryl shaped my new wig and I wore it to her birthday party held at the Dockside.

I wore my new red wig to the John Denver night at the club. Many friends didn't recognize me. Jill and Cheryl accompanied me to the Cancer Wig day. I was allowed to pick two wigs and a hat. We had fun trying on the different wigs. I also got a fleece green, red, orange, yellow plaid hat. I have had many compliments on the hat. It was a color I would have never picked for myself but it works with a lot of outfits.

The next scheduled chemotherapy was the 1st of August and Jill was my Gin (card game, not drinks) partner. She went home on the 2nd of August after my bone injection. Laurie and Jeff, friends that used to live in Sequim, had arrived, Laurie liked to cook and she did all the meals while I did the cleanup. We had a great thing going. We played golf and Jeff went fishing with Gill. Laurie spent the next two weeks trying to fatten me up. She made some incredible meals but my appetite was not there.

On the 10th of August my sister arrived at the Port Angeles airport for a few days. While she was with me I developed some mouth sores and she spent quite a bit of time trying to get me healed so I could eat. We tried the wheat grass but I could not chew and the wheat grass hurt, so I had to spit it out. We bought some stuff at Sunny Farms that was supposed to heal mouth sores. They didn't work. I used some canker sore medicine that helped but did not take it away soon enough. She made soup with my new blender so I could suck down my food.

We finally went to see the doctor and she gave me a prescription. Within two days I could eat again. I had ordered new china cabinets, and Sharon and Laurie polished all my silver so when the cabinets came, the silver would be ready to be put back. I was so very thankful.

Sharon and Laurie accompanied me to Cheryl's house to cut, thin and style my two new wigs. My favorite was the gray one, although many liked my wild red. Several people told me I should dye my hair red when it finally grew back. I didn't really think that was an option for me.

During this process of nausea and tiredness, Jill sent me some special medicine: pot

A little medical marijuana goes a long ways and I welcomed the appetite it gave me and how it helped with the nausea. I was having all sorts of problems with my bowels due to medication and the marijuana did not give me negative side effects.

On the 15th of August Cheryl accompanied me to my chemotherapy treatment. We played Gin and she brought lunch. We discussed the Ladies Invitational finalizing all the little details.

Jill arrived the next day before my shot. Afterwards, I arranged for her to play a practice round at SunLand Golf Club. Thursday was our Scramble on the back nine. We had a lot of fun and I actually played the entire scramble. We tied for third place. On Saturday we played again, and this time it was best ball. I was amazed that I could play the entire 18 holes. God was good. I had asked that he help me reach that goal and he did. We didn't win but I felt good being out in the fresh air.

Thursday, Debra, Derek and Lola arrived. Baby Lola was so cute. We had a big dinner on Thursday evening and Derek, Debra and Lola walked part of the way on the golf course watching Jill and me on Saturday. Debra and Lola joined us for lunch after the golf tournament. Lola was a good girl and everyone got to meet her.

After the tournament, we celebrated my birthday at SunLand. On Tuesday the 23rd my foursome celebrated my birthday at Mary Jo's house. Debra and Lola were our special guests.

Lola accepted her grandma even without hair. It took her a little while but soon she knew who I was. We went to the game farm and she was not sure of the big animals coming so close to the car but when we got to the petting zoo she was thrilled and wanted to pet every one of the animals. She was very happy. They all left on August 25th. I was sad to see them go. Lola made me smile.

We started a new drug protocol on August 29th I had no idea how this drug would affect my body so I was a little nervous. The drug was called Taxol. Cheryl wanted to be there for me for this new experience. The first thing they did before each session was to do a blood test, then we waited for the results. While waiting, they weighed me, took my blood pressure and I met with the doctor to discuss the tests and what that day would entail.

The first time taking Taxol was a long day. Quite a few people get an allergic reaction to the drug so they want the infusion to be done very slowly. They gave me 50 mgs. of Benadryl by infusion, which made my legs twitch and become very restless. I also got very sleepy but I couldn't sleep because my legs were bothering me so much. Then they started the Taxol drip. It was supposed to take 4 hours. Cheryl brought lunch and Gill showed up after his golf game. I finally started waking up a little more and we played cards. I didn't have a reaction to the drug so the next time they told me it wouldn't take as long.

Again I received the bone marrow shot the next day and had the same energy on that day. Gill was headed off to go fishing the next morning and I thought I would be fine. The doctor had given me a prescription for pain pills but told me not to take them unless I really needed them. The next morning I was in so much pain, I felt like a truck had run over me. My entire body hurt, even my bones.

Gill called later that morning and I told him I was definitely going to need the prescription filled, as I was miserable. He came home from fishing and got me the drugs. Unfortunately they didn't help much. I really hurt. The medication dulled the pain somewhat but I was not sure I would make it for the full two months.

After this experience I decided I would try the medical marijuana. The pain pills didn't work and the effects of the drugs caused constipation and then diarrhea and my body was all confused. I called my doctor and she had the paper work for me by that afternoon and Cheryl and I took off to Port Angeles to see what I could do about this problem.

Cheryl and I were a little hesitant as we drove up to the place. It was a very small facility. There was a policeman outside the door talking with a young lady. It turned out the lady was complaining about a person who had caused a disturbance at the facility and she was filing a complaint against that person. The marijuana people there were very helpful. They didn't have much stock but I left with enough to see if this would work for me. I was amazed at how many varieties of pot they had.

I took my new purchase home and after my next treatment I started in the morning and it made me calm, sleepy and hungry. I slept through much of it for the first three days and I was soooo grateful to have this new medication. I did not have the pain I had experienced before and knew that I could survive, thanks to the Marijuana. There are several types. Some is for pain and some is for nausea. All of it helps the appetite. I would recommend it for anyone going through chemotherapy.

The next chemotherapy session was September 12th. Marsha had volunteered to be my chemo partner and bring lunch. We played cards and the nurse told Marsha she should let me win and Marsha let her know that there is no way she could do that. Her competitive nature would not allow such a thing. The nurse laughed.

The nurse slowed down the Benadryl infusion so I didn't experience the leg twitching.

The Taxol was infused more quickly since I hadn't had a reaction with the last treatment. I was much happier not spending 7 hours with tubes sticking out of me. I had my shot the next day and smoked my marijuana the following day and life was better. I didn't hurt so much.

On the 26th of September Mary Jo was my chemo partner and the entire process went very fast.

Jill came the 27th of September till the first part of October to help Gill bring the boat back home to Sequim and put the new cover on it. She also did a lot of yard cleanup, weed spraying and general cleanup.

On October 2nd we all went to the Japanese restaurant to celebrate Gill's birthday.

Seventy years old. Time flies.

On the 10th of October my golfing foursome decided they would all show up for my last chemo treatment. It started at 8:00 am and they were all there to hear what to expect next. We played Shang Hai till the infusion was done. We were out of there by noon and we all went to my house for lunch and to celebrate that chemo was a thing of the past. I was very fortunate to have so much support.

My golf foursome

Left to right:
Marsha, Mary Jo, Cheryl
Me in front

CHAPTER 13
HEALING

The treatments were finished. My new protocol was a port flush and a doctor's visit every three months for the first year.

Denise arrived on Halloween and stayed for a week. She made some smoothies for me and we juiced vegetables for a healing green drink. I was grateful for her help and enjoyed spending the time with her. We froze some curry soup for a later date. Denise announced that her family would come to Sequim for Christmas. I had already decided that I was not going to spend one more month in this house so I told her I would not be here. I could not see decorating and getting ready for Christmas for a four day visit and then being stuck in this house.

On the 15th of December we left Sequim for California. We arrived at Debra and Derek's house two days later. Denise and Bryan had decided to go to her father and step-mother's house for Christmas and would spend a couple of days with us in Sacramento so we could see the boys. My grandson Joshua was in the process of making me a hat to wear. It fit perfectly and I wore it a lot. His brother Owen was working on a neck scarf that you could pull over your head but it was too small. He was disappointed but I was touched that he even tried. They are great boys.

The weekend was planned and the men played golf on Saturday and we all went to Alcatraz on Sunday and had dinner on Pier 39 in San Francisco. It was a fun day and the boys really seemed to enjoy their time on the island. Sunday night they were off to go snow skiing in Tahoe. I was thankful they gave me two days.

I just heard of a class at Stanford. The last lecture was on the mind-body connection and the relationship between stress and disease. The speaker (who was head of psychiatry at Stanford) said, among other things, that one of the best things that a man could do for his health is to be married to a woman, whereas for a woman, one of the best things she could do for her health was to nurture her relationships with her girlfriends. At first everyone laughed, but he was serious.

Women connect with each other differently and provide support systems that help each other to deal with stress and difficult life experiences. Physically this quality "girlfriend time" helps us to create more serotonin—a neurotransmitter that helps combat depression and can create a general feeling of wellbeing. Women share feelings whereas men often form relationships around activities. They rarely sit down with a buddy and talk about how they feel about certain things or how their personal lives are going. Jobs? Yes. Sports? Yes. Cars? Yes. Fishing, hunting, golf? Yes. But their feelings? Rarely.

Women do it all of the time. We share from our souls with our sisters/mothers, and evidently that is very good for our health. He said that spending time with a friend is just as important to our general health as jogging or working out at a gym.

There's a tendency to think that when we are "exercising" we are doing something good for our bodies, but that when we are hanging out with friends, we are wasting our time and should be more productively engaged. Not true. In fact, he said that failure to create and maintain quality personal relationships with other humans is as dangerous to our physical health as smoking!

So every time you hang out to schmooze with a gal pal, just pat yourself on the back and congratulate yourself for doing something good for your health! We are indeed very, very lucky. Sooooo let's toast to our friendships with our girlfriends. Evidently it's very good for our health.

After the end of my treatment, I sent a letter to all of my supportive girlfriends, sharing what I had learned from the study.

This study really exemplifies my situation and without you and your support the journey would have been DIFFICULT and at times unbearable. I cannot even begin to tell you how much the time you spent with me during the chemo treatments, changed the way I viewed my circumstances.

I was encouraged, fed, entertained, prompted to get out, eat more. You put up with my whining and prompted me to buy new clothes, and put on makeup, so I didn't scare anyone that came in contact with me.

I know that your care and friendship pushed me to a quicker recovery and a can do attitude. There are not enough words to express my gratitude. You saved my life and I hope I never have to do the same for you.

I pray for your health and blessings for the sacrifices you have made for me.

It has taken me a long time to write this letter. I wanted to cover all the blessings from my friends and thank them properly. I was so afraid I would leave out something because there was so much care and love poured upon me that I get overwhelmed. (I also claim Chemo Brain.)

You are truly God's angels. I always knew he had my back but was pleased that he used my friendships to carry out the details.

When I read this Stanford study I knew it was perfect timing for my THANK YOU LETTER.

I am progressing nicely and feel stronger each day. I feel the Cancer is cured and I am on the road to complete recovery.

THANK YOU

With my cancer treatment over, I was finally free to focus on other things. At the top of that list was my grandchildren.

My family decided I should have a birthday party to celebrate my 70th birthday. All the family came to Sequim.

I decided that it would be fun for all the boys to sleep outside in a tent. I had sleeping bags and flashlights for each of them. They set up their tent and got it ready for the night.

When I got up the next morning, they were all in the living room.

"Why are you in here?" I asked

"Grandma, at about four o'clock in the morning the sprinklers came on and we all got soaked".

I could not convince them to try it again. I told them I would make sure the water was turned off. NO WAY was their answer. They will never forget their outdoor adventure at Grandma's house.

They arranged a dinner and I invited several of my friends and family. The girls bought me a ring and it had all of the birthstones of my children and grandchildren. It was beautiful. The most fun was the treasure hunt my grandchildren sent me on. They thought up all the clues and numbered them.

1. The apple tree in the back yard
2. My fishpond
3. Vegetable garden that had a nasty weed called horsetail. Hard to get rid of.
4. Bird feeder outside my bedroom window
5. The golf cart in the garage. The kids loved to drive around my yard.
6. My mailbox. Inside was the package with the ring in it

The clues to your birthday gift begin here!!

1. You grow these in your backyard, & it's your favorite lunch snack with peanut butter. Go to your backyard for the next clue!

love: Owen

Congrats!! You found your second clue!

2. Your next clue hides among rocks that surround something you built from below the ground up. & you've fallen in it before. It's not far from where you stand.

Way to go Grandma!!! you found your next clue.

3. Your next clue is where a certain weed formed it's own underground cities. We spent hours digging it up. Go to this place for your next clue.

♥ Gabby.!!

Awesome! You made it to your next clue.

4. Birds congregate here to eat. outside a place where you can watch them closely.

Love always, Phia!

Well done! That was a hard one!

5. All the kids have used it, but now it's broken. It's even related to your favorite sport.

Love . Ash

Good job Grandma! Your only walk left is from here to where your birthday gift hides.

6. Your gift hides in a place where you get love from all over the states. Put some shoes on for the gravely walk to find it.

Debra and Derek decided they wanted to have another child. They didn't want Lola to grow up an only child. With some outside counseling, they decided they would do an in vitro pregnancy.

Many people told Debra she was getting a little too old and the possibilities of having a child with special needs becomes higher the older you get. With in vitro they can check the fertilized eggs and make sure they are healthy. Debra and Derek started the process and came up with four good eggs, all healthy and all boys. They had two implanted and now they had to wait. Would they take? Would she carry the babies full term? How many would remain viable?

They got the news that none of the eggs took and she would have to start over. My answer from the very beginning was that, God was in charge and he would decide what baby they would or would not have. I encouraged Debra to put her faith in him. If it was a special needs child then so be it. There is always a reason. A few months later she was pregnant and nervous about carrying it full term and healthy.

Mikell Burk was born October 30, 2013.

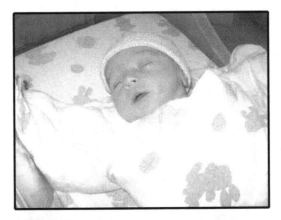

I was always so fortunate to be at the birth or within days of the birth of all my grandchildren. I found it quite rewarding to help, cook, babysit and welcome the new family member.

I have to admit, as I got older, I got a little more tired.

Being a grandmother is truly one of the greatest blessings in my life. I was once told that grandmothers are antique little girls. I have so much fun playing with my grandkids. We run around, play board games, go to the movies, color and do just about anything they want to do. One of their favorites is a game of chase that I start out by saying FEE FI FO FUM I'M GOING TO GET ME SOME CHILDREN and that is their signal to run. I chase them and when I catch them they get tickled and hugged and kissed. They run through the house screaming and laughing. Their parents don't always appreciate our noise but they know the kids are happy. The two year old recently told her mother, "When grandma comes back, I'm going to tickle her." My purpose is to create memories. The older grandchildren are too big and I couldn't catch them if I wanted to. They actually miss the game.

Another one of my traditions is to make fudge for Christmas. I send it or bring it to the children when I come to California. This was a tradition my father handed down and taught me how to make his special fudge. He would ask us if we were free to crack some walnuts, as this was in back in a time when we would get the walnuts in the shell. We knew what was coming and cracked those nuts in no time at all. We liked it when he would test the fudge to see if it had reached the softball stage. This process was done with a small bowl of cold water and he would drop a small amount of fudge in the water and if you could make it into a soft little ball, it was ready for the next stage. We got to sample his tests. My mouth is watering just thinking about his fudge. I make it but it will never be as good as his.

Chapter 14
Perspective

Over the years, when having a conversations with someone telling me, "That's your opinion" or "That's your perspective," I kept wondering what it really meant. How did that help me communicate? I didn't know how to address the conversation because it seemed to end there. I asked the Lord to help me figure this out so my conversations wouldn't be stopped dead in their tracks.

I was mowing my yard one day and as I came around to the front yard I was admiring the berm that ran two- thirds across the front yard. The shrubs were blooming. The lavender was beautiful, the poppies were scattered all across the front. I was in awe of the beauty and thanking God for the gift of my yard.

A little while later, I took my dog for a walk and as we went down the street, I got a good look at the other side of the berm. It was not pretty. All of a sudden, I got the message. The Lord told me that in the conversations that led to "that's your perspective," we were both right. It just depends on which side of the berm you were looking at.

Now I knew that all I had to do was ask a question. How did you arrive at that opinion or perspective? Then the conversation would be open for me to describe my side of the berm. The conversations could continue and maybe I would gain insight to their way of thinking.

We all have opinions and sometimes they are not true. We learn from our parents, from our friends. We are formed by our traditions, the decade we grew up in, and the experiences we've had. We all have our own perspectives on things. I have learned to listen more, ask more questions and have respect for other perspectives.

As I have written before, we were a Coast Guard family. We moved around a lot. We lived in many different states and another country. Because of that, we were able to witness, first hand, different traditions, manners, ways of life, what other people deemed important and what they thought trivial. It was an education in itself. My children learned so much and because of that they are not narrow minded or racist.

My family also experienced a lot of trauma with Michelle's death and how many people responded to them at school. Teach your children to be respectful.

That said, I have developed some perspective based on the experiences I have had. Many of which have been covered here in this story, but I have also developed a sort of "Mission Statement" based on what I believe. The two greatest areas in which I have honed my perspective are parenting and faith.

Parenting

My mission as a mother was to raise children to become responsible adults. It was not to make them my best friend or to give them everything they wanted. I made it a point to say what I mean and mean what I say. If I said "no" it did not mean maybe. If I gave a warning that "if you do that one more time you would get a spanking," (yes spanking was allowed in those days) I followed through. They always knew I meant it. There were not many spankings because the warning was enough to discontinue the bad behavior. I took care of the problem immediately. I would hear my friends say, "just wait till your father gets home." I used to shudder. Poor dad had to be the bad guy.

The girls would have to pick up their toys when they were finished playing and clean up their rooms. They were given jobs to do around the house for an allowance. Their jobs included: rake the yard, do the dishes, empty the dishwasher, empty the wastepaper baskets, take out the garbage, put your laundry away. Depending on where we were living, there were other responsibilities. They earned money and could spend it anyway they liked. I had the jobs lined up on a rotation basis so no one could say that they always got the worst jobs.

It was important that they learn manners. Please and thank you was at the top of the list. Being a military family they learned to say, "yes sir", "no sir" "yes ma'am" "no ma'am". They were not allowed to call any adult by their first names unless that adult told them otherwise. Table manners were difficult because their father insisted they learn to eat as though they were in a fancy restaurant. Many times he would hit their hand with a fork when they tried to eat with their fingers or talk with their mouth full.

A major lesson we wanted them to learn was to always tell the truth. They had to learn the hard way. If we caught them in a lie the punishment was doubled. If they told the truth, many times the punishment would be cut in half. Most of the time their punishment was some form of restriction.

Rules and regulations were good but I also believed in having fun. We went to beaches, concerts, ice-skating, and to the Kennedy Center for Christmas fun. We had so many adventures in Japan and Hawaii. Many times I was complemented on my children's behavior. I knew I could take them anywhere. I don't believe in all work and no play.

We always taught you should have enough money in the bank to carry you for three months in case you lost your job or got sick. I think they follow this teaching and have never borrowed money from us.

Denise, Bryan, Josh and Owen continue to live in Walled Lake, Michigan, They travel quite a bit and are in the process of remodeling their home.

Debra, Derek, Lola and Mikell live in Sacramento, California. They both work full time and enjoy their two young girls.

Jill, Lon, Sophia, Joey, Jack, and Lexi all live in Salinas. They are all involved in the 4-H club and raise animals to show and auction at the fair. Gabriella, their eldest daughter, is attending Sacramento State College to become a preschool educator.

All of my daughters own their own home with either a pool or a lake in the back yard. They have goals for their lives and their children's lives. The children are being taught work ethics. Nothing comes free. They make me proud to be their mother and grandmother.

This does not mean that I did everything perfect or without mistakes. I made choices I now wish I had made differently. After Michelle's death, I should have been more aware of their trauma. I should have sent them to counseling so they would have someone to talk to. They didn't want to talk to me because they didn't want to make me cry. Many years later they told me they had not only lost a sister but had also lost their mother. I had emotionally shut down. But then I discovered the simple act of forgiveness. It is a simple solution of letting go of blame or anger or guilt, but one that many don't want to tackle. People often think they have a right to be angry or bitter or resentful, and that may be true, but all they are doing is hurting themselves. Once I realized this, a big load was lifted and life was bearable again. Forgiveness--of myself as well as other people--took away anger, bitterness, stress, and brought me the peace that passes all understanding.

My daughters are themselves all mothers now and understand the love a mother has for her children. Sometimes they asked how I survived. I remind them that Jesus was always with me and even in the middle of the most difficult storm I survived and I want the same for my children and grandchildren and the generations to come.

Which leads to...

Religion

Many different people have told me that all religions were the same. I know this is not true. I once heard that the definition of religion, was man making the rules to get into heaven, while Christianity was God/Jesus reaching down to us for a relationship. No one is perfect and no one can do enough good works to get into heaven.

Who will free me from this life that is dominated by sin and death? Thank God! The answer is in Jesus Christ our Lord. (Romans 7:24b-25a NLT, second edition)

I once heard this testimony of a Chinese Christian:

I walked through the road of life and had fallen into a great ditch. The ditch was filled with depression, discouragement, and sin. As I lay in that ditch, Mohammed came along and said, "It's your fault you're in the ditch. You offended Allah, and this is your just punishment." Then Marx came by and said, "You're in the ditch because of class warfare. You must revolt." But after the government changed, I was still in my ditch. Then Buddha came along and said, "You're not really in that ditch. You just think you're there. It's all an illusion of the mind. Be at peace, and learn to live in your ditch." Then Confucius came by and said, "Here are the 10 steps of self-attainment by which you can get out of your ditch. If you will struggle, you will climb out eventually." But as much as I struggled and strained, I couldn't get out of the ditch, because it was too deep.

Then one day, <u>Jesus Christ</u> came by and saw me in my ditch. Without a word, he *took off his white robe and got down in the muddy ditch with me. Then he lifted me up with his strong arms and pulled me out of the ditch. Thank God that Jesus did for me what I could not do for myself. Jesus did for you what you could not do for yourself.*

If you want healing in your life, you have to believe that Christ can change you. The answer to your problem is a person. Who's going to be lord of your life? Who's going to call the shots? You or Jesus Christ? When you're mastered by him, you can master your problems. God has the power you were lacking. He'll help you out. (Author Unknown)

Someone once asked me if I would rather live as though there is a God and be wrong, than to find out in the end that there is a God and I didn't surrender to him. I personally know there is a God. I have witnessed many miracles and he has brought me out of the deepest sorrow. When you accept Jesus as your savior and surrender your life to him, it is as though the curtain has been lifted and you have a new understanding of who Jesus is and what he is about and why we need him. The Holy Spirit comes to live in you and shows you the way that is right and acceptable. The first thing we must do is surrender all to him. He cannot guide us if we hold on to our stubborn ways and want to do it our way. Trust me, God has a better plan. I pray that all my family and friends will find the path to GOD through JESUS CHRIST and have victory in their times of trouble.

Jesus doesn't expect us to be perfect. He teaches us from the inside. He changes our heart. He helps keep out bitterness and the desires to get revenge. The bullies of this world are so insecure that they have to lash out at someone else. It is the only way they can feel important. Jesus loves us unconditionally. Come and see for yourself. You won't be sorry.

I hope to be the official greeter in heaven when it is your time to join me.

Debra Denise Jill Me

Jill's 30th Birthday

Debra Jill Denise Me

Our trip to Alsaka

family trip to Lake Tahoe

Epilogue

There is a new storm brewing. I feel it headed my way. Because of my faith, I am not afraid.

God is in control and I have witnessed how these storms can impact others as much as it impacts me. God is working on reuniting my family.

I had not been feeling well for a little over a year. I had had several tests with no definite results.

Finally I was given a new CAT scan and it revealed a growth in the uterus near the ovary. I was given special blood tests to see if the tumor was in the ovary or colon. The results came back high for ovarian cancer. I was given an ultrasound and scheduled for a hysterectomy. When I finally saw the doctor in Seattle he told me I couldn't have the surgery because a couple of lymph nodes outside the uterus were malignant. They would have to reduce the cancer in order to make the surgery safer for me. The lymph nodes were the problem.

It had also spread up into the stomach lining. I was told that I would have 6-9 weeks of chemo and then have another CAT scan to see how much the cancer had been reduced. If it had reduced enough they would schedule surgery to remove the uterus, ovaries, lymph nodes and parts of the stomach. They were also concerned that there might be some bowel involvement so I would have a bowel prep before surgery.

The port was installed and I completed my first 9 weeks of chemotherapy. The surgery was scheduled for the 26th of October.

The doctor was not sure if there was any involvement in the bowels. I would have the clean out drink the day before surgery so they could have a better look. No colonoscopy just the prep.

Two different antibiotics were prescribed and I would be having a shot in the stomach every day for 21 days after surgery to keep blood clots from forming.

An EKG was ordered, to make sure my heart could take this surgery.

Two days before the surgery the doctor called and informed me that I had an aneurism in my brain that had been discovered 5 years ago. It was a shock to me. No one had ever told me about this. She said she could not do the surgery until a new scan was done and the doctor needed to approve the surgery. The scan was done and the doctor reported to us that the surgery was the most important priority and needed to be done. The aneurism could be fixed at a later date.

The surgery was performed on the 26th of October and lasted about three hours. They removed the female organs and parts of the stomach lining. They left the lymph nodes because the chemo had reduced the size of the cancer. They could not get all the cancer because it had spread into the bowels in little finger like extensions. No tumor, just small amounts throughout the bowels. I was in the hospital for 3.5 days.

I was so blessed to have each of my three daughters take turns coming up to Washington to take care of me after surgery. They fed me, they nagged me to drink more water and eat more food and that is exactly what I needed. They hovered over me making sure all my needs were met and the house was kept clean. They came by age, Denise was first, Debra was second and Jill was third. They escorted me to chemo and appointments after surgery. What would I have done without them.

I was put back on chemo three weeks after the surgery. I will have 9 more weeks and tested again to see how much cancer has been killed. An added drug has been suggested for this kind of cancer but the question is still up in the air about the aneurism. The new drug, Avastin, raises the blood pressure and with an aneurism you don't want high blood pressure. The question is: do we fix the aneurism first or monitor the blood pressure while taking the new drug.

I have decided to take the new drug to kill the cancer now. I can't have surgery for the aneurism until all the cancer treatment is done. I know GOD has my back and he is in control but I have to admit, this process is so long that it overwhelms me.

And yet, in the midst of uncertainty and treatment and constant medical appointments, I was given one of my biggest blessings. My wish and my prayer was for my family to all come to Sequim for Christmas, 2016. We have never been all together at the same time. There are fifteen family members and a lot of logistics getting to Sequim and finding places to stay. My house could not accommodate fifteen extra people.

The Lord had a plan. One of my friends loaned me a house that was empty, fully furnished and quite large. It accommodated the three daughters: Denise & Bryan, Debra & Derek with their two little girls (Mikell, 3 years old and Lola 6 years old), and Jill and Lon.

The four boys, Jack, Joey, Joshua and Owen—all a few months apart at ages 15 and 16—stayed in my guest house and the three girls, Gabby (age 24), Sophia (age 18), and Lexie (age 12) stayed in my room. We had a blow-up, queen-sized bed for them, and Gabby slept with me.

The girls did all the cooking and cleaning and we ate well. It was so much fun and everyone had a great time. The kids went to the river and the game farm and played Heads Up in the evening. There was much laughter. Gill set up a Pickle Ball tournament for all the kids and adults and they loved it.

It was absolutely perfect, and I couldn't imagine it being any better. Someone asked me if I was sad when it was time for everyone to go home. I had to say "no," because I was so grateful for how wonderful it had all been. In the middle of hardship, I am still given this gift.

I call this my MIRACLE CHRISTMAS.

Keep the prayers coming.

Carol Goodman
January 20, 2017

Back row: from left to right. Joey, Owen, Denise, Joshua, Bryan, Lon, and Derek
Middle row: Gabby, Jack, and Debra
Front row: Jill, Sophia holding Mikell, me with Lola in front, Lexi, Gill with Mayling

CHAPTER 15
GILL'S CHRISTMAS LETTERS

The purpose of the Christmas letters were to let our friends know where we were each year and what was going on in our lives. The letters are funny and unique. They were Gill's attempt at comedy with exagerated stories of each of the family members. He always got approval from the girls before the letter was sent out. One of the letters was written by Debra and I wrote a few to give Gill a break. Enjoy.

1979

DECEMBER 21, 1979

MELE KALIKIMAKA !

It's that time again and no one at the Goodman house can comprehend where 1979 went. Time does go fast when you are having fun. Please accept our slightly late, but still enthusiastic, wishes for a VERY MERRY CHRISTMAS and prosperous NEW YEAR. We had high hopes for getting our Christmas cards in the mail by 5 Dec. 1979 but Gill ended up in Leadership school and Carol accompanied him on a little side adventure to Lake Tahoe/ Reno. (Would you believe the Blackjack tables paid for the trip? It's true. Great way to wind up a delightful year).

It is impossible to list all of our activities for the past year but maybe just a few comments to bring you all up to date.

General:
Hawaii is the greatest (Weather, life style, outdoor activities. In addition, we had the pleasure of seeing lots of visiting relatives and friends who we haven't seen for ages. If your schedule & travel funds permit - come visit us in 1980.

Gill:
Hairline holding it's own (C.G. Record: Bald spot and nose sunburned 37 times in one year.).
Stopped answering telephone (of the 2510 telephone calls received at the Goodman house in 1979 only 2 were for him.)
Has to look up to Michelle and Denise'sboyfriends ((contemplating use of elevator shoes and Afro haircut).
Loves job and living in Hawaii.

Carol:
Has 3-4 jobs to take up her spare time (?) - (Tax Consultant, Amway Distributor, Supermarket Demonstrator, etc., etc.,)
Instead of 5th daughter has adopted a female Shih Tzu puppy named Mayling. (Gill's comment - "As soon as first telephone call is received for the dog; telephones will be disconnected.")

Born Again Christian (recommends this path for everyone - especially mothers with four daughters and golfer husband).

Michelle:
Still smiles occasionally.
Outgrew Carol's clothes 3 years ago.
Starts legally driving next month (parents are contemplating purchase of Sherman tank as training aid).
Went to first high school Senior Prom in April (Gill's comment "Have a good time but be home by ten." Michelle's retort "Generation Gap"!)

Denise:
> Smiles constantly.
> A hard working & diligent student.
> Had her first night time date in Oct. (boy took her to carnival, spent $15 on her and Denise couldn't remember his name the next morning.
> Outgrew Carol's shoes last year.

Debra:
> Hasn't stopped talking since last Christmas (no relief in sight).
> Our input to C.G.A. class of 1991.
> Loves to compete on coed soccer & basketball teams.

Baby Jill:
> All-time con artist. (for example been known to say, "I think all good looking brown eyed people should get ice cream. Right Dad?" Gill's comment "Hard to refute that type of exacting logic, Carol - more ice cream for Jill and I".

> Took longest unauthorized trip of year (played hookey from school and took the Bus to Waikiki (45 Minutes) to take in the action).
> High Scoring soccer forward.
> Easter's pet chicken grew into a 3 foot mean fighting rooster. (Hawaii Zoo officials were called upon to remove from premises).

All in all it has been a fun filled and rewarding year for our clan with only two regrets:
> We didn't get to see/visit with all our friends.
> N.Y. Giants wouldn't be in the Super Bowl.

We hope that both regrets are alleviated next year.

Until then - again - MERRY CHRISTMAS and a HAPPY NEW YEAR.

LOVE & BEST WISHES
GILL
CAROL
MICHELLE
DENISE
DEBRA
JILL
&
MAYLING

1980

1980

(Author's Note: In my Position Description there is a small item near the bottom of the list that says, "Write Christmas Letter." This year, for various reasons, I procrastinated and spent a lengthy period meditating at the golf course. After considerable pressure from my publisher I got to work. I'm sorry about the delay and can offer only one solid excuse; artistic license.)

TO ALL - MERRY CHRISTMAS & A HAPPY HOLIDAY SEASON

All events during our past year, of course, have been overshadowed by the loss of Michelle in a tragic automobile accident. She is gone to a better world but will never be forgotten. Since she was God's gift to give and take, who can question the wisdom of it all? But we are most thankful for the 15 years she spent with us and feel proud and honored to have lived with and known this special child. Her memory lives with us all and we are confident we will be better people for those wonderful years.

We are still living in Hawaii but it is tough! We strongly concur with the recent Commandant Coast Guard decision to declare the Hawaiian Archipelago a hardship area. It is impossible for mainlanders to understand the boredom of waking up every morning to sunny ($70-85^{\circ}F$) weather, the disappointment of not being able to choose which tie or winter coat to wear, or the repetitive trips to the store to get suntan lotion, golf balls, surf board wax, etc.

Gill, being the most adaptable, is probably surviving the best. By sheer determination he overcomes the biweekly visits to the golf course (handicap 6-7), struggles through the 4-day, 10-hour/day Coast Guard work week engaged in an interesting job, and suffers through the simultaneous sunbathing/NFL football viewing. It is inconceivable how much this man can endure.

The kids, being young and unknowledgeable, fare next best - Denise has developed into a teenage flash and honor-roll student. It is hard to imagine the metamorphosis from the 4-year old "grubber" into a scholar, but in 10 years it happened! For a period there we thought the CIA had recruited Denise. She was wearing so much makeup, she had to be this year's version of Mata Hari. It was too much to observe - this head with its eye liner, rouge, lip ice, flakey hair-do, etc. on top of an old sweatshirt and farmer's style blue jeans. Recently it's been the Cheryl Tiegs well-scrubbed look with dresses. How quick the changes occur. Hard to keep up.

Debra is still our all-American kid. A determined child ready to take on the world; which includes parents, teachers, sisters, homework assignments. It is a pleasure watching her beat (either physically or verbally) her newest boyfriend into submission. Our overall assessment is: "Watch out world here comes Debbie."

Baby Jill usually brings up the rear but not on the soccer field. Still small and delicate but a tiger as center forward (six goals in her last two games). Wearing glass has corrected a slight astigmatism. Her first statement after donning her fashion-conscious eyepieces was "Daddy, you're going bald." Gill hid her glass for week.

Carol, now a blond, is still expanding into new ventures; tax consultant, Amway supervisor/ saleswomen, Born-Again Christian and still looking for other areas of interest. All this and mother to the "terrible trio" is a tough assignment. Her biggest problem is that there is not enough hours in the day. Submitted a beneficial suggestion that in the next life days are 36-hours long.

Mayling, Our lovable Shih Tzu, still rules the roost. No way to outsmart this little rascal. During her 2-month pregnancy received overwhelming attention and concern. When she figured she had pushed it to limit declared the whole thing a false pregnancy and recommended returning to ops normal.

We all wish you all a Merry Christmas and Happy Holiday season - And if you get a chance please come visit us in paradise -

Best wishes to all —
The Goodman's

1981

TO ALL - MERRY CHRISTMAS & HAPPY NEW HOLIDAY SEASON   Dec 1981

It is that time again. A period of the year which we think
should be enjoyed to the fullest but it is also a time to reflect
on the good things and the wonderment of it all. (As with each year
the past one has been both happy & sad for the Goodman clan. On
the very sad side was the passing of Carol's Father who now joins
Carol's Mother and Michelle in a place where the beer is always cold
and the trap shooting is always perfect. He, like the others, will
be sorely missed but never forgotten. A loving Father, Grandfather,
and good friend.) My editor says I'm late again! But what the heck;
she said she wanted a Christmas, not a Thanksgiving, letter. To each
we wish a Merry Christmas, Happy Holidays, and a continued success
next year.

Life in Hawaii continues to be blissful although we have had
our moments. Today, for instance, it is cloudy and the temperature
has plunged down to 72°F. Days like this just drive you crazy.
All the tourists are stuck indoors and they spend their time trying
to take photographs of us local Hawaiians or just listening to us
talk. Why just yesterday at an Oahu drugstore a mainland gent said
to Gill after a 20-minute conversation, "Gee your accent sounds like
you grew up on one of the other Hawaiian Islands." Gill retorted
with "Yea Brah, Manhattan." Still a small price to pay for perfect
weather, golf/beaches year around, no ties, flip flops everywhere,
etc. Before we discuss some future plans a little local news from
the past year:

Gill made a big mistake asking Carol to play golf. His handicap
went up and hers is going down. Playing golf with women was never
his best suit.
All the girls played soccer again this year. Denise's team
won first place. Debbie and Jill are going to Maui to play in an
all star tournament. Santa is giving them plane tickets with a
little extra spending money.
Denise is in High School this year and struggling to keep her
priorities straight between studies and social life.
Debra in Jr. High and doing very well.
Jill in 5th grade has the teacher conned with her sweet smile
and big brown eyes.

We bought a Camper Van so we could do some traveling and visiting of old friends and family next summer. This will make good
material for a book. GOODMAN'S CAMPING?
Gill is beside himself, after 20 years of rooting for the
Giants they have finally made the playoffs. His faith and loyalty
has paid off.

Word has it that the Goodman clan will be leaving paradise
next summer as the great wagon train moves eastward. For sure
there will be a culture shock and moments of depression when we hit
the mainland. But nothing lasts forever. Since no one is sure
where our next assignment will be, The Great Sanweinee (i.e., Gill)
has implemented a comprehensive training program to prepare his wife
and "hogs" for any eventuality. For example:

NEXT ASSIGNMENT	PREPARATION DRILL
Boston	Carol sits nude in the refrigerator two hours/day playing with ice cubes.
Washington	Gill sits daily in a parked car (simulated traffic jam) for 2 hours, then goes to the local amusement park and spends an hour

1982

Happy Holidays and Best Wishes to all our Friends,

Many of you (my wife included) will probably think this year's Christmas and New Year's letter is late. Not true! Since I have taken to observing Chinese New Year (13 February) this letter is, in reality, early not late.

For us the past year has been filled with those events that alter and illiminate our times. First and foremost we relocated from the islands to Southern California. This was done for two reasons: first the Coast Guard determined that after 6 years outside CONUS the Goodman clan had developed borderline native tendencies (The coup de grace was when the Admiral observed Gill at Mess Night in full dress with flip flops! At least his toenails were polished.) Second Carol got a message from on high that the first typhoon in 23 years was due to hit Oahu - Time to go. The overall family consensus is that Southern California is acceptable but we have noted the following:

1. People talk funny. No one understands "Mo Bettah, Like Slaps, Stink eye". Jill sayes she hasn't understood anything her teachers have said since school started.

2. Automobiles move fast. If they moved that fast on Oahu they would run out of island in 15 minutes.

3. It is cold. Gill went outside in his bathing suit in September and froze solid. Carol removed his suit and now he is a statue adorning the front lawn.

4. Air is not always clear. Ever stroke a 10-foot putt and have to determine success by sound not sight?

5. Everyone eats funny food. Where has all the sushi, poi, tempura, won tons, pineapples, and coconuts gone?

6. Everyone wears shoes. Heck of a way to go thru life! Don't mainlanders love their toes?

Well enough on the obvious differences and a little about the local Goodman clan news:

Gill(59) - A new job (CO, Base Terminal Island). An interesting and different type job. The reason he got the job was due to his medical record. The assignment officer noted numerous record entries alluding to "terminal senility" and so for Gill's next assignment just matched first words.

Has become a devoted aerobic participant at the local health club. Lost 15 pounds last month just by sitting in a chair watching the bevy of young ladies jump around. When he gets home each night has to stick his fingers in the wall VAC outlet just to get his heart started again. A real health freak.

Carol(38) - Back home in California again. Has spent the last 5 months landscaping/painting the outside of the house. Is now a "world class" wheel barrow operator. Considers herself Orange County's expert in type and quality of manure. (Heck the rest of us knew she was a horse s--t expert years ago.) Received a personal thank you letter from President Reagan for her efforts to reduce the balance of payment deficit thru excessive purchases for house restoration. She now uses phrases such as "quality of life" to explain away her uncontrolled procurement impulses.

Denise (16) - Insured Bell Telephone showed a profit for the past 5 months. Candidate for debtor's prison in Georgia. Could have traveled to Hawaii for the money she spent calling there. Has developed into a good looking, personable, scattered-brain teenager. Recently required a two-phase extremely-complex medical operation to have her Walkman headphones surgically removed from her ears and mattress removed from her back. Completed her undergraduate work last night at dinner with the following question for Gill; "Since you have an opinion on everything, what do you think about premartial sex?" The Heimlich Technique was required to remove the taco from Gill's throat.

Debbie (13) - An outstanding student. Her keen intellect and sense of humor in the classroom has significantly improved the promotion possibilities of junior teachers in both Hawaii and California by causing many elderly (her definition: anyone over 25) teachers to seek retirement or another field of employment. Another teenager with her feet solidly on the ground. A "world class" Pac Man and Donkey Kong performer. Has repeatedly informed both parent that based on knowledge acquired during recent school sex education courses she is available for consultation if either of them have any problems of a sexual nature. Gill honestly believes that her training bra is too tight which has reduced the supply of oxygen-filled blood to her brain.

Jill - (12) A nice stable young lady who has recently commenced developing dreaded teenage tendancies. From the number of telephone calls made/received during the past 3 months she must also have stock in AT&T. The proverbial con artist who plys her talents on everyone. Went to her first dance and had a great time. Carol reminded her beforehand not to punch out her dance partner regardless of his comments or dancing ineptitude.

May-Ling (4) - Our loveable longaired Shih-Tzu. Tough time adapting to the cold Southern California climate. Over last 2 months has gained 15 pounds due to her reluctance to go outside to do her business. Presently looks like an appendix ready to explode.

As you can see I take these holiday letters very seriously. But really, the entire Goodman clan is having a good time and hope all our friends are enjoying. We think of you often and hope we can all get together very soon. Please come visit if possible. Hope you had a Merry Christmas and Best Wishes for a Happy (Chinese) New Year. We are all praying that you have a safe, successful, and happy 1983.

Until we see you -
Best of Luck,

1984

7 December 1984

HAPPY HOLIDAYS & BEST WISHES TO ALL OUR FRIENDS;

I would like to take full responsibility for failing to accomplish all of my assigned duties last year(i.e., neglecting to produce my annual Holiday letter). During this past year I have taken much verbal abuse from many of you all due to my oversight. Although it is nice to be remembered, the language you all used to describe my slight transgression will not be soon forgotten. I have an excuse that I'm afraid many of you are unaware of!! During the last holiday season I underwent a serious, complex operation; full body cosmetic surgery performed at the UCLA Medical Center. I am now a "larger than life" cross between Boy George and Tom Selleck. The winter/spring 1984 were spent at a Hollywood drug store waiting to be discovered. I even went so far as to submit a VCR tape of Carol and I in the raw for audition purposes. As you probably have figured out by now this "Boy Selleck" of the Coast Guard was not chosen for a film career. (I was hoping for a full-length porno flick or at least a travelog with Farrah.) Somehow the Commandant got wind of my surgery and decided that an "early out" from the LA area was in the best interests of both Boy Selleck and the Coast Guard!!.

We accepted with some disappointment last summer's unscheduled transfer to San Francisco. We are now residing at the DOD Housing Facility, Hamilton AFB in the heart of affluent Marin County (just north of San Francisco over the Golden Gate Bridge). The following is the results of last night's voting: Gill-would rather be in Hawaii, Carol-Southern California, Denise-listening to her Walkman, Debra-Huntington Beach, Jill-doing her nails, MayLing-2 barks and a scratch. As you can see the family is presently undergoing that rough readjustment period that occurs just after moving. During our short stay in San Francisco we have noted the following:
   1. Although the song "It never rains in Southern California" is untrue, with respect to rainfall San Francisco should be considered Seattle South vice LA North. Even the golf balls are mildewing.
   2. San Francisco's & Marin County's scenery is spectacular. A uniquely beautiful area.
   3. Whoever said "I have never been as cold as during a summer day in San Francisco" knew some stuff. (I think it was Vanessa Williams.)
   4. Gill carries a sign which sayes "HETEROSEXUAL - DO NOT TOUCH!!" whenever he gets on a crowded BART train. Better safe than sorry.
   5. The kids say, compared to Southern California, their fellow students in the Marin County schools are all hillbillys/beatniks/etc.. A prime example of the continuing Southern versus Northern California arguement. (Personally I think all California is the "Cereal Bowl of the Pacific"—You know nuts and fruits on top of a bunch of flakes.)

Well, enough of that and now a little local Goodman clan news... (Please note regarding the news of our teenagers I have provided the necessary translation in parenthesis for the adult readers.)

Gill (59) - A new job (Chief, Telecommunications Management Division; USCG Pacific Area) whose most difficult aspect so far is figuring out what to say (or not to say) at the biweekly staff meetings. Strongly believes his long-held theory is definitely correct—the longer the job title the more insignificant the job really is. Enjoying the golf in Northern California-waiting to return to Monterey for a week of uninterrupted golfing. Long term goal: reassignment/reemployment/retirement in Hawaii.....

Carol (38) - Back home in Northern California again. Disappointed in having to leave her enjoyable "interior landscaping" job. Spending her time getting the new house outfitted and organized. During the past year got lots of time on the golf course (best score 83, lowest handicap 16). Enjoyed holidays (which included golf) at Palm Beach, FL and Hawaii.

Denise (17) - Involved in her last year of high school in Southern California (translation: maintaining a low profile hoping no one will count credits). Debating over whether to commence her PHd studies at MIT/Stanford or enter the business world in search of her first million (normal, undecided teenager tiptoeing from cloud to cloud).

Debra (15) - Reasonably well adjusted teenager (translation: her number of spoken English words greater than or equal to number of grunts). A chip off the old block (inherited her father's big mouth and her mother's irresponsible financial tendancies). Continues to actively support the Supreme Court's decision on breaking up monopolies (keeps all the various telephone companies in business). Spends all her spare time in her room studying (writes alot of letters to boy friends). Unique personality (enjoys pissing everyone off at least once a day). Astute teenager (a relative measure, sort of like Pittsburgh's division leading record in the AFC Central this year).

Jill (13) - Has not yet fully developed all the dreaded teenage characteristics (translation: only argues with her mother once a day). Acknowledged as the best cook in the house! Must be constantly cautioned by her mother to ensure training bra isn't on backwards otherwise the little devils might be trained to start growing out of her back. Recently announced that she intends to live with parents until she gets married at 30 (translation: expects to mooch for another 17 years-both parents spent the rest of the day trying to shake the depression).

MayLing (5) - Still center of attention..Is not sure she enjoys the colder, wetter weather. Has taken a strict vow to refrain from sniffing other strange dogs while in this sexual liberated area!!

Enough of this trival stuff — The Goodman clan wishes a Happy Holiday Season and 1985 to you and your loved ones.. Be safe, successful, and enjoy!!

UNTIL WE SEE YOU—
BEST OF LUCK,

Gillo

Debbe

Carol

Denise

Jill

May Ling

117

1985

1 December 1985

HAPPY HOLIDAYS & BEST WISHES TO ALL OUR FRIENDS;

For the second year in a row, I have overcome the dread writer's block and accomplished the impossible: getting the Christmas letter out early. To tell the truth it was easy this year because of my present position which is not too demanding to say the least... This job leaves much time to develop racquetball skills, browse in the exchange, read the sports page, etc., so finding time to write a Christmas letter was small potatoes. As a matter of fact, I have repeatedly suggested that my present position be abolished as the beginning of a Coast Guard-wide cost savings initiative. But as I was told by the hierarchy: It is impossible to delete your billet because all staffs must have at least 10 Captains (O-6s) or we wouldn't be able to hold fully sanctioned Coast Guard staff meetings which require at least 10 Captains in attendance and breathing although none have to be awake. (Note: I have taken this rule to heart and have slept thru the last 25 staff meetings without any noticeable adverse side effects.)

Biggest news with the Goodman clan is not what happened in 1985, but rather what will happen next summer: retirement from the Coast Guard, career change, relocation to Monterey, CA! This evolution will permit testing of Gill's long held theory: "In my next life I'll pick an area I'd like to live and then look for work instead of allowing the job to determine the geographical area." Although all family members are excited/happy about the proposed move, none are quite as ecstatic as Carol. Being a Monterey resident for 25 years and then leaving for a decade or so has certainly strenghtened her resolve to return to the scene of her youth. We are all wondering if she will ever run out of stories about little Carol Saunders and sister Sharon. In any case, the new adventure starts soon and the answers to the following questions and more will be the subject of future correspondence:

    1. Can Gill find happiness and fulfillment as Mr. Mom?

    2. Will success in the real estate business spoil Carol Goodman?

    3. Should Debbe and Jill be permitted to date the sons of Carol's old flames?

    4. Do the Monterey Police still have Denise's picture on file from the time she, at the age of two, ate the neighbor's dog food and then bit their dog?

Well, enough of that stuff and now a little local Goodman clan news....

Gill (balding) - Because of his Academy background/military smartness, has become known as Captain Kangaroo. Deeply involved in preparing for a second career by using all available resources (e.g., community colleges, correspondence courses, etc.). Has determined that being a successful house husband will not be easy but intends to give it his best shot. Recently scored very high in the annual Women's Day house husband test. Magazine evaluator was particularly impressed by his exceptional reaction/performance in the following areas:

    a. NFL Football - Spent an entire Sunday afternoon bitching at and berating spouse for wasting time watching grown men trying to injure each other. Then left house to attend a dynamic arts and craft class in pine cone painting.

    b. Soap Operas - Demonstrated action above and beyond by watching 4 continuous hours of the soaps without a head call. Ate entire box of chocolate-filled cherries during All My Children and called Erica a bitch seven times.

    c. Sexual Favors - By rolling his eyes just so, ensured spouse understood she would not get near him that night if she drank one more beer.

Although scored high on all house husband tests, results indicate that he could improve in the following areas: complaining that no one seems to care if the kitchen is clean, being unreasonable for a week straight once every month, gossiping, etc..

Carol (39) - Excited and extremely happy about starting over in Monterey. Presently studying full time, preparing to take her California real estate exam in January 1986. Intends to manage (or possibly sell) residential property. Does not intend to stay home every day with Captain Kangaroo when he retires. (Says his squirrel factor has gone up 1000% in the last few years.) Actively involved in aerobics, bridge, golf, and house hunting. Delighted to receive all her clothes back from daughters who have now all out grown her size.

Denise (18.8) - Attending college/working in Santa Barbara. Developed into a dedicated college student (will wonders never cease). Top salesperson in an avant-garde men's clothing store. Her sales routine to all young male customers combines the usual "fits good in the front" with the bull only a good looking young lady could get away with, for example: "That shirt is you", "Makes you look so Don Johnson-like", or "I love it and I'm sure your girl friend will also". Gag me with a spoon!! Says between school, working, and beach volleyball hasn't got time for a serious love life. Carol hopeful situation remains status quo for at least 3 years.

Debbe (16) - Note name change. Accomplished in accordance with existing Marin County directives. Parents happy she did not think of "Moonbeam", "Dawn Light", or "Summer Warm" first. Dynamic, intelligent, deaf high school junior. Recently cited by Los Angeles Police for excessive radio noise erupting from her new car while parked in our northern California driveway. Her criteria for car selection in priority order: speakers (must have four big mothers), radio/tape deck, paint job, horn, seat covers, glove compartment, and finally engine/mechanical considerations. Always cash poor but retains her expensive tastes. Awarded 1985 1st Team All Marin County honors as high school soccer player. Plans to attend University of California Santa Cruz and major in engineering, economics, soccer, and buff males. (For all you ancient types, "buff" these days means well built not sans clothes. Thank God.)

Jill (14) - With practice and extreme determination has developed into a typical teenager with all the inherent pluses and minuses. Super athlete!! Report card looks like middle of the alphabet. Extremely helpful around the house except for her own room which is an acknowledged disaster area. At the end of a long and busy weekend, a doctor was called in to surgically remove the telephone from her right ear. Very excited about going to Monterey as move will permit her to compare her marks against her mother's grades at the same school (i.e., Monterey HS). Believes no way she can lose since she recently discovered some of her mother's old report cards. Her first comment was "How could you have taken typing when they didn't even have electricity then?" Her wardrobe makes Auntie Mame look like a conservative wimp!!

May Ling (6) - Can't wait to move to Monterey. Has had it up to here (about 3 inches off the floor) with the unisexual sniffers in the Bay Area. Says if you have met one sniffer, you have met them all. Blames Coast Guard for destroying her love life as she quotes recent Playdog article noting that Bay Area's available heterosexual male dog to female dog ratio is lowest in nation. Intends to seek employment as a long-haired artist in Carmel. As it maybe her last chance before doggie menopause, plans to "jump the bones" of one of Clint Eastwood's male Shi Tzus immediately upon her arrival in Monterey.

Well enough of this trival gossip.... The Goodman clan wishes you all a Happy Holiday season and 1986. Stay safe, be successful, and enjoy!!!!

UNTIL WE SEE YOU AGAIN -
BEST OF LUCK,

Gus Carol Debbe Denise Jill May Ling

1986

23 December 1986

HAPPY HOLIDAYS & BEST WISHES TO ALL OUR FRIENDS:

This year before rehashing the annual news I have a very important disclosure to make....This revelation became necessary when I read the latest National Inquirer's English Literature section headline "Gill wins Pulitzer for his annual Christmas letter." That coupled with the realization that many readers were complimenting Carol for her writing efforts has made it imperative that the following important facts be made public: Carol can't write her way out of a paper bag, the only English Gill is familiar with is the small print on the bottom of beer cans, and the girls are only big in love letters.... It has been me, May-Ling (the loyal Shih-Tzu), all along that has observed these events and every year taken paw to word processor to get facts on paper. Writing this stuff is the easy part; these bozos provide plenty of material. The tough part is finding a word processor and chair built for us little hairy people... So, in the future, don't compliment skin head, the silver Castor Canadensis, or the harem if you like the letter but rather send expensive doggy bones.

This year was an important and eventful for us: retirement from Coast Guard and relocation to the scenic and beautiful Monterey Peninsula. It was accomplished without incident during February and unanimously declared an unqualified success. Relocation required the usual good-byes and development of new friendships. Easier for some than others. But as this holiday season approaches all Goodmans are well situated and progressing nicely.

The sporting event of 1986 took place in June; The first annual Goodman Golf Open. Such great SOCAL sticks as DJ Aites, Jim Culbertson, Ray Pratte, etc came and made their charge. Not every participant was a par golfer but all were definitely scratch drinkers. For those who were sober enough to remember; Carol lead after the first day, but choked and allowed JC Dust Bunny to steal the grand prize.

Now for a little local Goodman news.........

Gill - Found employment as Project Manager for an electronics service contract operating throughout central/northern California. Requires traveling a few days a week which is a godsend for the rest of the family but has detracted from his life long ambition of being "Super Mr. Mom". Is extremely despondent over the lack of time to devote to his house husband duties such as ironing, washing windows, servicing the mate, etc... Still bossing everyone around (I hate it when he orders me "Drop it quick I'm freezing out here". Spent 2 months trying to teach me to use the indoor toilet but my tush is just not shaped right and they didn't have any current doggie magazines.) His new job requires that he work twice as hard as he did when he was in the Coast Guard... But, of course, that is still half as hard as the normal person. After 20+ years of frustration has witnessed his NY Giants making a serious bid for the top. Every Sunday morning he dresses in his NY Giant uniform complete with helmet and spends the hour before kickoff practicing his NY accent and mugging prevention techniques...

Carol - For the 5th consecutive time awarded California's Non-Cook of the Year Award. Spent early 1986 house hunting. Was determined to find a 4-bedroom, 3-bath house without a kitchen. After 3 months without success accepted the fact that the house would have to have a kitchen but immediately drew up plans to convert it into a 5th bedroom. Developed the now world-famous "Monterey Diet" which simply consists of visiting the Goodman's for a 2-week period and eating with the family. Now a successful real estate agent but spent the summer doing volunteer work at Carmel's Century 21 office. Becoming reacquainted with a multitude of her old friends.. Having a ball!!!

Denise - Successful college student in Santa Barbara. Considering transferring next year to San Diego State. Must be nice to get educated at all the California vacation spots. Has set a all-time Denise record by going with the same fella for 10+ consecutive months.. The grubber has grown up!!

Debbe - High school senior whose future plans include college at Santa Barbara or San Luis Obispo to obtain one of the following degrees: elecrical engineering, urban/city planning, Mrs.... Manages the pro shop at the local raquetball club. Spent a major portion of last year arguing with her boyfriend but recently declared a Christmas truce (a la Corazon Aquino/communists insurgents) which made the other shell shocked Goodman residents very happy.

Jille - Another teenager who has decided to change the spelling of her given name. Strange individuals these adolescents. (Carol swears to take a 5-year respite after they all leave before ever becoming a victim of the empty nest syndrome.) High school sophomore whose future plans include becoming a high school junior. After two unsuccessful attempts to pass her driver's test believes the third time will be a charm. Saving all her spare money to purchase a new Toyota 4x4 pickup truck; now has $55 available for this procurement.

Myself, I love Monterey!!! I've cured my slice and am now a 8 handicapper from the doggie tees. In 1986 I hope to meet Charles Schultz's Snoopy and jump the bones of at least one of Clint Eastwood's male Shih Tzus. Until that eventful day I remain your faithful keeper of the Goodman news......

All the Goodmans hope you have a wonderful holiday season and may 1987 be the best there ever was!!!!!!!

MAY-LING
        for
            GILLO, CAROL, DENISE, DEBBE, JILLE

1987

31 October 1987

Season Greetings to All Our Friends!!!!

Editor's Note: Being a lazy fellow I put the word out -"A big $50 or bag of doggie chow for anyone who will write this year's Christmas letter. The following is the only thing received (Believe she might have some talent but she certainly is verbose and I'm not sure about her sense of humor(?).):

A happy October to the very patient friends of the "Goodman Clan". This year's NEVER ON TIME GOODMAN CHRISTMAS LETTER will be written by the sanest, probably most intelligent, and definitely most punctual member of the family, Debbe. (Even the dog is getting too old for this task.) This year I have decided to write in October (i.e., the month of my birthday for those of you who forgot or just neglected to be giving) so that this letter would arrive early instead of the following February. Sometimes I wonder if my father even knows which month Christmas falls in. It's December, Dad. (He is going to "edit" this as if he'd even know what a grammatical or spelling error was!) Now that I'm almost on my own (well socially, NOT FINANCIALLY) it's time for me to assume some responsibility and take over (at least for this year) the writing of the annual Goodman February letter.

The Goodman Clan is doing extremely well! I'll start with the oldest:
    Last year's author May-Ling, now 56 years old, had her first college experience. The folks left the hairy one with me for a week. She thoroughly enjoyed herself but felt it was a vacation that lasted too long. You know the kind! Remember 7 doggie days, that's almost two months for you and me!
    The Retired Captain is the next eldest on the list. We try to remind him each and every day that he IS retired and has NO authority. He is doing fine physically, and even financially, but as for mentally, the volume of air between the ears is increasing rapidly. (Maybe the brains leave as the hair goes. Yes, he still combs the little hair he has over his ever increasing bald spot.) I knew something was wrong when he visited me at college and slipped me a twenty. This is the same man who thinks us girls should take off 50 pounds and shrink a few feet so that we can wear the same old girly clothes he bought us 10 years ago. Recently bought a Boston Whaler so he can relive his youth sailing the mighty oceans of the world. The family decided he was "losin' it" when he grossly miscalculated the quantity of decorator rock for the front planter. When the huge dump truck arrived, we ended up with three times the rock needed. (Pops - A cubic yard is 27 not 9 cubic feet!) Now not only are the flowers surrounded by decorator rock, but also the trees, plants, grass, and even weeds.
    Next up is Mom. Probably the youngest at heart. The silver Castor Canadensis is the hardest worker in the family and I'm sure she will one day be rewarded for all the work and "extras" she has done for everyone. I had to give her one of those daughter-mother talks the other day about "making it" in a career. Her temper got away from her when our Yuppie next door neighbor decided to do some loud drilling in his backyard at 6 AM after his dogs had barked past midnight. It wasn't a pretty scene when she went barreling out of the house to give him a piece of her mind and from the absolutely foul language she used she must have given him a piece of Dad's mind too. I advised her that if she wanted to climb that Century 21 ladder of success she had better think twice before giving anyone a piece of Dad's mind.
    Then there's Denise. She is now attending San Diego State down there in the city of "new Mexico". From what I understand she is enjoying herself,

meeting new people, playing   soccer, and studying.(Probably in that order.)
When she explained to me that she can't afford to eat anything other than
popcorn, I thought it would probably be a good idea to invest in a meal plan
at my college dorm.

The baby of the family has definitely grown up. Jille is now a driver
and awaiting a car (Probably from the car-fairy.) She has a job at a local
restaurant and hopes to save enough money to buy a car. I've decided that
she shouldn't buy a car just yet. I told her she should wait until she is
eighteen. Why you ask? Well, at the present time she is renting my car for a
$100 a month while I'm down south sun-bathing; I mean studying. (I keep for-
getting Dad is going to edit this letter.) At this rate in about 2 years or
so the car will be paid for again and I could sell it and make a hefty profit. Then while Jille can barely afford a Pinto I'll be driving a brand new
Porsche. If Jille's nice, maybe I'll sell her my car. I might have to work
on convincing Jille that it's a good deal. (I've already convinced my Dad,
but then again he thinks I'm going to pay him back for college.) Jille has
been getting good grades at high school but has decided to pass on a college
engineering degree because she wants to keep her children safe. Confused,
read on. My Pops, being the great engineer, designed a pully system to re-
load the bird feeder that hangs in a tree 30 feet off the ground in our back
yard. After he had a few beers, he hired Jille to help with the construction
phase. Upon completion he filled/raised the bird-feeder, patted himself on
the back many times, and directed Jille to pick up all the tools. She told
him the feeder was probably going to fall but he patted himself on the back
again and informed her that the bird feeder would still be up there in 20
years. As Jille stood up after picking up the tools, wham, and she fell flat
on her face. The pully system's rope had broke and the bird feeder fell 30
feet down square on the top of Jille's head. She was out cold. When she
awoke on the couch with a headache I was at my client's side explaining her
rights as an accident victim. From that day on Jille wants to be as unedu-
cated as possible. Then her children will not only be safe, but they will
also be able to play on the front lawn instead of the front "rock patch".

Last but not least, there's me. I know I'm a little out of the "oldest
to youngest" sequence, but when it comes to bra size, I'm definitely the
youngest in the family. In fact, I'm the youngest girl in any American family with girls over twelve. Well, I never have to worry about anyone "bor-
rowing" my bras. I've started my first year at the University of California
in Santa Barbara. Sounds pretty important eh? Well amongst us locals the
college is known as UCSB (i.e., U Can Study Buzzed). I look forward to being
the first accomplished college graduate in the family.

Well that's about it for this year. I hope each and everyone of you that
reads this letter AND ENJOYS IT has a great Christmas and an even better New
Year. For those of you who don't enjoy it - may your New Year's resolutions
be broken within the first month leaving you with guilty feelings for the
remaining 11 months. And for all of you, if you'd like to come and visit
Monterey between the months of September and June (not including the Thanksgiving, Christmas, or Easter vacations) the Goodman household has a room for
rent. The family has conveniently left me to handle all the financial details (I'm in the book). Stay healthy and enjoy the forthcoming year.....

Debbe Goodman

1988

25 December 1988

Season Greetings to All Our Friends!!!!

As you can see the big day has arrived and the Goodman clan is busy opening their presents. How those bozos can carry on! So while they are squealing and hugging each other I've taken the opportunity to sneak away and prepare this year's Christmas letter. Personally I'm a little disappointed with my presents this year. Just how many stupid doggie sweaters, artifical chew bones, or boxes of flea powder does Monterey's Shih-Tzu sex symbol have to suffer thru. Heck my letter to Santa asked for some cosmetic surgery (you know a fanny tuck and face lift so at least the male dogs can tell which end is which) and a life size nude picture of Benji. Well anyways I'm back in my traditional role as the author of the annual Christmas letter. Last year's exper- iment was a mistake; allowing a college student to do anything except study, drink beer, and mooch $$ from their parents is counterproduc- tive. It is really just that one is much more observant to their sur- roundings when one's nose is just a few inches higher than the doggie messes scattered here and there. (Early mistakes and few baths teaches that our failures stick with us for a while.) Enough said on that!!

The Goodman clan is continuing to do well in Monterey. Those that were married before are still married and those that weren't are still not. Got that? OK, see I've still got it. Now for a little Goodman news - pay particular attention because there will be a quiz at the end. Top student will get those damn artifical chew bones and the flea powder.

Gill - Captain Kangaroo is still employed as a Project Manager for various electronics service contracts in the California area. During the past year opened a marine electronics (sales & service) facility in the Monterey marina... Better fisherman (many salmon and other slimy things this year) then he is golfer (a 7). Spent many hours out on the Bay communicating with the fish. Goes sort of like this: "Please fish nibble. If you bastards knew the crap I take from my wife when I go home empty handed you'd jump in this boat.". Spent a November weekend climbing every tree on the left side of the Bayonet's 4th hole (bet- ween 125-140 yards out). Seems he lost his 8 iron when it became a "helicopter" after he missed a shot and air mailed the offending uten- sil... All and all a very strange individual and getting worse.

Carol - The silver Castor Canadensis is a cross between Roseanne and one of the Golden Girls. Ran unopposed and of course successfully in winning her seventh consecutive California Non-Cook of the Year award. Never ceases to amaze me how the woman can screw up dry doggie food.. Still in the real estate business. Has almost convinced old Baldy to sell the house considerably below market value just so she can get the commission.

Denise - Still living on popcorn at San Diego State. Celebrated her 21 birthday in February. (Debra, with Denise's ID, spent the night out on the town celebrating in Santa Barbara while Denise with no proof spent

the night at home in San Diego watching Moonlighting. You figure it
out.).... Parents define each year of this college experience as an
annual 9-month party with an $8000 cover charge.... Personally I think
this college thing is vastly overrated. I've yet to see a doggie hunk
with a college degree.

Debra - Has returned to the traditional spelling of her name. Into her
second year at UC Santa Barbara. Decided engineers were too weird and
switched curriculums to business/ecomonics. Wants to be future Chair-
person of the Federal Reserve System. Says learning about money beats
learning about neutrons/electrons or sitting in science labs any time.
Has survived the rigors of college life and the annual Santa Barbara
Isla Vista Holloween bash (35000 people in one square mile) without
major injury. Although recently developed right knee ligament problems and the Doctors directed she abstain from all physical activities for 6 months. Debra then reluctantly gave up dating for that
period (?). The world's worst driver! Has yet to back up any vehicle
without doing damage to objects behind her. Neighbors have increased
all possible insurance coverages.

Jille - Now attends Monterey Academy of Hair Design. (Spends off
moments swapping Academy stories with her father. He relates about his
days sailing the Eagle and she tells intriguing tales of pedicures and
perms.) Attended more school in first week (6 days @ 8.5 hours/day) at
beauty school than she did her junior year at high school... Brilliant
child. Had her first unauthorized party at the house while the parents
were gone - Drank all the old man's Coors and replaced them with
Schaeffer hoping Baldy wouldn't notice... After a major disagreement
(knock down brawl) with Debra ran away from home - Parents were very
sad! After a few weeks of living out on her own Jille returned home -
Parents were even sadder!! Recently announced that she intended to
live at home until she was 25 - Carol immediately began receiving shock
treatments for extreme mental depression!!!

May-Ling - I'm still cruising along running this house. Nothing escapes
my watchful eye.. Based on my sustained outstanding performance during
the past year believe it is about time for a salary and perk review.
Think I'll push for an extra week of vacation so I can go to Palm
Springs and scam some doggie golf pro while enjoying the rays. Next
year think I'll change occupations. Sure would like to model some
doggie underwear. I fancy myself as sort of the canine answer to Jim
Palmer... Until you see me in Women's Wear Daily with my tush covered -

Hope you all have had a very happy holiday season and the whole Goodman
Clan wishes you the very, very best for 1989....

        May-Ling for
                Gill, Carol, Denise, Debra, and Jille

1989

8 January 1990

Dear Friends,

I know, I know I'm running late again. But this year I have a good excuse for my tardiness. As only my close friends have been aware, for
some time I have been going blind. For the longest time my vanity and
that macho black and white sniffer from down the street prevented me
from doing something about my condition. Luckily for me in October my
young love interest bit the dust trying to urinate on the garbage truck
during an up cycle. (He has been known ever since as Monterey's first
astrodoggie.) When that happened I finally decided to take some action.
After weighing the alternatives I applied thru proper channels for a
seeing-eye person. Would you believe a year wait for a properly trained
seeing-eye person unless the applicant could provide their own trainable
dummy. No problem, Old Baldy volunteered and spent one month undergoing
rigorous training. He is wonderful now at crossing streets, sniffing
lawns/other dogs, etc. but damn since he leads we have spent the last
few months at numerous golf courses, racquetball courts, and 27 gin
mills. Old habits are hard to break but this coming year I'm determined
to get my seeing eye person to Carmel for shopping, the opera, ballet,
etc.. Well enough; using the braille typewriter provided by the silver
Castor Canadensis lets get to another year of exciting Goodman news.

For the Goodman clan this past year has been absolutely outstanding with
lots of fun. Although some things remained status quo (e.g., still residing in Monterey, girls in college, Gill's compassionate/sensitive
personality, etc.), many new adventures were attempted and successfully
accomplished. (First for those who are interested and also the remaining
99% that don't give a fat rat's ass (which category includes their
beleagued parents), during the past year all the girls changed steady
boyfriends. Carol's comment was "When you get real serious bring the
poor bastard around for us to meet."}

A little general Goodman news:

All survived the big earthquake of October '89. The house shook/rattled
but sustained no damage. Jille was home at the time and became a true
believer on the spot. Carol was driving around Monterey and actual witnesses later testified that it improved her roadmanship. Gill was in
Alameda (approximately 5 miles from the overpass that collapsed) playing
racquetball and had just hit a "photon" forehand when all hell broke
loose. His playing partner (CDR Richard Burke) captured the moment for
all in the attached excerpt from his forthcoming book, "Travels with
Little Dick". Denise and Debra in Southern California stated both their
margarita blender and boyfriends give off more action (?).

The older Goodmans purchased a new Grady-White 22-foot boat which has
been named "Carol's Jag". For the uninitiated this is the ultimate
fishing machine which will be severely tested during next year's salmon
and albacore season. The boat is presently undergoing shakedown cruises
under the watchful eye of Captain Carol. And where is Old Baldy? He
occupies the same position as he did on the CGC Absecon during 1963-65;

that of JOOD (under training). But it will be his job to navigate the
vessel back to foggy Monterey from the albacore fishing grounds (30-50
miles offshore). He has taken this responsibility very seriously; re-
viewing his celestial navigation and aligning his Loran-A receiver.
Since I am not an old sea dog and need grass to do my business I have so
far been spared these lengthy nautical adventures.

Another piece of major news: Carol is now an executive. She was promoted
to CEO of Century 21's Seaside office. She is responsible for the management of the entire office and its 8 real estate agents. Baldy has
been giving her the benefit of his many years of management experience
imploring her to use such phrases as "The buck stops here", "It is
lonely at the top" and of course in true Coast Guard staff tradition to
have more meetings and write more memos. Probably the best indicator of
her management style can be derived from the name her subordinate agents
have coined for her; "Hitler's sister".

Specific Goodman news follows:

Gill - Capatin Kangaroo is still screwing around and enjoying himself in
the electronics business; opened an Oakland marine electronics (sales &
service) business for the parent company. Loves that salmon fishing and
golfing (a 6) in the Monterey area.

Carol - Would you believe the old gal has hidden talents as a fisher-
person (last season caught 2 salmon for every one Old Baldy did). Spends
at least one day a weekend pursuing those slimy ocean things. Goal this
year is to win the annual 3-day Monterey Salmon Derby. Became a blonde
in the summer. Then after the first week whatever Jille did went wrong
and only the bottom half was blonde, the top was a sick orange. Jille
thought it was great now that "Mom's a punker!!". For the next 3 months
the neighbors and her real estate associates just looked in amazement.

Denise(22) - Due to graduate from San Diego State in May. Will wonders
never cease? At this point the most stable, mature of the offspring although there is a story circulating about her sleeping way on
top of a pool table in a fashionable Santa Barbara bar. (Baldy was in
the process of reading her the riot act when Carol reminded him of those
long past European cadet cruises; he went away sheepishly.)

Debra(20) - Red shirt junior at UC Santa Barbara. Had an exciting year
learning how locks work. First locked up her bicycle with the "ultimate
burglerproof" lock and lost all the keys (that bicycle has been recently
declared a state monument in front of her apartment). Saved the best for
last: While home on vacation during an evening rush hour pulled in to the
busiest gas station in downtown Monterey, waited in line till her turn,
then got out to pump gas and realized she had locked herself out of her
car. Effectively blocked half the station for 30 minutes until Carol
could get there with the spare keys. Made alot of friends!

Jille(18) - Due to graduate from Beauty school in the spring. Set a
family record by moving out of the house three times in the same year;
unfortunately each time she came back. Carol says the next time she

leaves the old folks will sell the big house and move into a one bedroom condo. Ha gotcha!! Finally conquered mathematics (or at least count- ing) at a Lake Tahoe blackjack table. Says the hell with new math just give all the kids $50 bucks and a deck of cards. Went orbital when those dealers busted.

May-Ling(74) - Still sniffing along checking them out. (Eyes might be bad but I have the quickest nose in town.) Had a very enjoyable Christ- mas vacation in Lake Tahoe with the rest of the Goodman animals. Really enjoyed the ski slopes. No I did not do any actual skiing since all dogs have recently been barred from the slopes. (Seems the authorities are blaming a few of my fellow doggie skiers for leaving messes half way down the slopes. Before it freezes I guess it is quite an experience to hit that stuff at 50 miles an hour during a downhill. Tough to get it off your goggles.) But I did love the apres ski in the lodge. Scammed on alot of furry hunks. And you should see my new ski outfits. Those spandex pants really do something for my tush. Love it!!

Hope you have had a very happy holiday season and the whole Goodman clan wishes you the very best for 1990....

May-ling for

Gill, Carol, Denise, Debra, and Jille

1990

Better Late than never
Happy Holidays

19 December 1990

Dear Friends,

As with all years, 1990 was a year that brought both the bad and the good: First the bad news - during November the Goodman clan lost their #1 beloved hairy daughter/sister and the world lost a prolific writer on the level of Hemingway, Steinbeck, etc.. Yes Mayling left this world for a better place which she writes is a true Shangri-la; filet mignon with no worry about cholesterol, doggies always get the preferred tee times, Cleveland Amory writes only about man's best friend, and the New York Giants win every Super Bowl. (Baldy signed up immediately.) Second the good news, Carol was so despondent that she received an early Christmas present - a black and white female Shih-Tzu puppy named Mayling Too. That's good news in itself but an added benefit is that the new puppy can't read/write yet so this year's letter will bring that living legend out of retirement. Yes, that's right, hold the applause down, Super Baldy will again bring his concise, brief, no bull style of prose back for this year. Since this is a onetime shot may I suggest that you all tuck this letter away somewhere where it will be safe because for sure it will be worth megabucks in years to come!

Well after all that crap there is really nothing much to report that hasn't been stated adequately in past Christmas letters. So what I would like you all to do is go get that file of the past ten years of Goodman Christmas letters and reread them. After that review I can skip directly to those events that make this year unique from those past.

All the Goodmans are doing their thing, hopefully with determination and a flair to be remembered. The parents working hard at several jobs to make a living and give the best to their children. They sacrifice continually to ensure their offspring have all the things and chances that they themselves never had. If you saw Carol and I now you would see an older couple stooped over from the load, wrinkled like raisins, but proud of their ungrateful "yuppies in training" daughters. Parents out there - Don't you just love that kind of stuff??? I always wanted to write that just to make the kids squirm and to become the #1 hero for parents all over the world. The guilt trip. I love it.. Well I guess I got side tracked. At my age the mind wanders. Happy Halloween. Oops wrong letter!

For my money the sporting highlight of the Goodman year definitely occurred 3 June 1990 on Monterey Bay (approximately 1 nm off Fort Ord). Debra caught her first Salmon; a 42.5 lb monster after a 35 minute fight with 15 lb test line. It was the biggest salmon caught in the entire Monterey Bay by anyone (commercial or sport) for the past 7 years. Debra and her catch received Monterey Herald newspaper front page pictorial coverage. (For comparison sake the following is offered: During the April 1990 3-day Monterey Bay Salmon Derby fished by over 700 expert fishermen the winning fish was 27 lbs. (PS - Carol came in 17th overall (#2 woman) with a 21 lb minnow whereas DJ and I were skunked but consumed our limit plus some in frosty liquid refreshment.))

Gilly - Still plugging along in the electronics business trying to make ends meet. Golf handicap and waist line going up (10 and 34 respectively) and quantity of hair and sexual appetite declining (just like the Kinsey Report said). Makes out a new will once a month just to keep the smart mouthed daughters in line. (At one time last year had a will in effect which left everything to The Society for Gay Rooster Research.)

Carol - Top rod and reel performer out on the Bay womanhandling salmon and those big 6-foot blue sharks. Changed real estate agencies during the past year but things are so slow in that business no one has noticed yet. Spends an inordinate amount of time training the new puppy and again the positive improvement is so minimal that nobody has noticed. She says better things are ahead in 1991.

Denise (24) - In May graduated from San Diego State University with a degree in communications. Can now talk reasonably intelligently on a few subjects. Has remained in San Diego working in sales for a large sporting goods manufacturer/distributor. Has an apartment, new car, and no $$$. Number one boyfriend recently left town to pursue a professional soccer career in Detroit. Giggles at the idea of relocating to Midwest.

Debra (21) - In October the extended family convened in Santa Barbara for an historic weekend to help Debra celebrate her 21st birthday in style. It was a weekend full of those events/happenings that make lifetime memories. Of course the significance of the occasion was lost momentarily when Denise and Jill pull a "double moon" in the well lit, packed parking lot of the dance hall at 0200 closing time. I was completely taken back by such truly unacceptable and obnoxious behavior whereas Carol could only yell "let it rip, girls". (The Silver Castor Canadensis has really got to stop sipping Thunderbird.) Back to Debra - Almost done at University of California Santa Barbara (six months to go). Has interned for the past 2 years in the Goleta Water District. Appears that her efforts will not be in vain as she is now known throughout Central California as "Ms. Water Conservation" and will probably be offered a pretty good job in that field upon graduation.

Jill (19) - Changed from Beauty school to working in the Accounts Receivable department of major Monterey automobile dealership. Recently moved back into the Goodman casa. (Which, by the way, is up for sale -- The older twosome bought a condo on the edge of Monterey.) Did spend 6 months living in her own apartment. Her banking experience is probably indicative of that period. Her checking account with one bank was so screwed up that after spending two weeks trying to balance it she took the "Jill alternative" which consisted of throwing the bank book in the trash and opening a new account at another unsuspecting bank. The only 19 year old that carries a beeper so she won't miss any of her social calls.

May-Ling Too (3 months) - Sharp teeth. Good sniffer. Fast Runner. Intends to write Christmas letter in future.

Hope you have a very happy holiday season and the whole Goodman clan wishes you the best for 1991......

080
Mayling too   Jill   Carol   Jill   DeSn
                                         Denise

130

1991

16 December 1991

Dear Friends,

With lots of happenings this year and a break in my busy schedule; an early Christmas letter is in order... I'll be the author again this year as my relief, the little hairy one, is still in Doggie Summer School relearning sentence construction, punctuation and the like. Maybe next year??? Aside from the disturbing fact that we are all a year older, there is no bad Goodman news. All things considered it was a pretty exciting and quick-paced year... It started in April when we sold our large house and bought a condo within the confines of "Q-Tip Country Club". (Called Q-Tip because it is primarily inhabited by older people who have white heads and thin bodies; you know "Q-Tips".) Our little country club has a small 10-hole golf course, swimming pool, etc. and all the members call me "Sonny". It is a quiet place half way between Monterey and Salinas approximately 7 miles from our old residence... The year came to an end with Carol and I off to Las Vegas to participate in a golf tournament and gambling experiment. (We lost both but had some fun.) Well get a firm handle on your seat and let me quickly rehash this year's events and happenings:

Denise (25) - Married Brian Finnerty in September. Honeymooned in Maui. Now living in Michigan while Brian performs goalie duties for the Detroit Rockers, a professional soccer team... Wedding held in the fashionable Dana Point Resort was an event that ranked right up there with Woodstock. To the best of my recollection, midway thru the reception the entire wedding party and several key Resort employees ended up in the swimming pool fully dressed; to the astonishment and delight of several hundred other Resort guests (who were not involved in the wedding). During this unscheduled swimalong, the Resort's Head of Security sternly informed me "that the serving of all alcoholic beverages will terminate immediately." Seemed to me a little heavy for violating the bathing cap rule. Later on that night I noted that all the swimmer's tuxedos (mine included) had shrunk. Every male in the wedding party looked like he was dressed in a short sleeved coat with bermudas. Hopefully the tuxedo rental shop will have some future occasion to rent those particular tuxedos to a wedding party composed of alligators (you know, big bodies with little tiny arms and legs.) Not my problem. In any case the wedding was a Happening!!!

Debra (22) - Graduated from University of California Santa Barbara with a BS in Economics. Accepted an outstanding position as Water Conservation Coordinator for the City of Marina (8 miles north of Monterey) at a salary far in excess of her present abilities... Decided to do some postgraduate work at UCSB enroute to Denise's wedding. Too bad the course chosen was BeerTasting III. Her nighttime laboratory work was interrupted by Santa Barbara's finest and she spent the rest of the night behind bars allegedly for "Battery of a Police Officer". (This type behavior is reminiscent of her Mother's deportment at a similiar age.) I being the confirmed pacifist engineering a coup and the bogus charge was unceremoniously dropped. Unlawful confinement law suit pends. William Kunstler to be retained... Not to be outdone by her sisters, Debra got engaged in June and then upon further consideration/reflection got unengaged in July. Tough to keep track of...

Jill (20) - Being the great athlete it was no surprise that she caught the Bridal Bouquet at Denise's wedding. But what was surprising was the sense of responsibility that she felt for this honor. Jill got married 4 weeks later to Joey Santiago and lives in Monterey. She is working as a beautician and waitress buying furniture and all those other things young marrieds require. Joey continues to slave at Macy's following the American dream. Both are hoping for a quick lottery hit or similiar windfall. I say congratulations but don't quit your daytime jobs.

Mayling Too (1) - Extra special dog. Great athlete who is now in Doggie Summer School working on her SAT scores to ensure eligibility for next year's college soccer scholarship.

Carol (XX) - Dormant Real Estate Agent... Has became the family's golf enthusiast/champion (handicap 13). Played on the Fort Ord's women team and ended the year as the 2nd best Fort Ord woman golfer. She says next year intends to take it one step further and win the club championship. Had the champ on the ropes this year and let her off... The Silver Castor Canadensis spent 2 months redoing the newly-purchased condo. Seems the previous owners had a major blue fetish (blue walls, blue carpet, blue toilet seats, etc.). Even old salts could not enter the condo without taking dramamine and putting a patch behind the ear or it was feed the fish, over the rail time.

Me - Turned the big 50 in October and now eligible for all senior sporting events. Continue to play a little basketball and golf with a weekly ocean fishing expedition thrown in. Has became an avid racquetball player with (if I do say so myself) considerable success. It is a pleasure spotting a good young player 25 years and then kicking some butt. (Maybe The Last Tango in Monterey?).. Still doing some electronics business but working only 3 days a week... Performed my civic duties spearheading the adoption of the new San Francisco Ordinance outlawing blondes from wearing miniskirts within the city limits. (It appears in some cases their testicles were showing.)

Well enough for another year. To the two fine young men joining our family we offer a warm welcome but don't say I did not warn you - The Goodman clan makes the Adams Family look and act reasonably intelligent. Good Luck!!!

To all our friends we say have a happy and safe holiday season..

GILL CAROL DENISE   DEBRA JILL MAYLING TOO

1992

13 December 1992

Dear Friends,

It is that time again. The Holiday Season; a time for gift giving, party-
ing, and the annual "Christmas" letter. Everything appeared ready to go
this year until two weeks ago when our prospective author declared herself
a free agent. Mayling Too is presently evaluating a host of outside
offers. Our standing offer of high quality food, a warm place to sleep,
etc. is far down on the list. She sayes that a doggie's playing career is
short and you have to get what you can while you can. Hopefully she will
regain her senses in the near future, in any case, I'll write the letter
again this year.

The Goodman's enjoyed another great year in 1992: Lots of good and very
little bad.... All events were overshadowed by the birth of Joey and
Jill's first child; Gabriella Michelle Santiago (1419LT, 19 November 1992)
and their gaining custody of Joey's other daughter; Jessica Elizabeth
Santiago (15 months old)... Plenty of little girls in that house.. Reminds
me of years past. And so the cycle begins again. Glad to be on the outside looking in!! Now for a little rehash of this year's events:

Jill (21) - Undoubtably Goodman's 1992 Woman of the Year. Before the
arrival of the two aforementioned little girls, we celebrated Jill's 21st
birthday in Las Vegas. Since she was pregnant at the time serious party-
ing was kept to a minimum. The highlight of the 3-day vacation was dining
at Bally's world famous buffet. The place was packed and we were halfway
through a lovely dinner when Jill started to feel sick and raced in terror
for the nearest door. How was she to know that that was the door to the
kitchen. When she lost it the cooks' screams could be heard for miles.
(Ranked right up there with Bush's Tokyo dining experience.) Gabriella's
birth was a standing room only event attended up front and personal by
Joey, Carol, and Debra while I sat in the waiting room. Carol even video
taped the entire event with her new Camcorder. Now when we have a slow TV
night, guess what! So far I have fainted twice sitting in my favorite TV
chair and we are not even to the summer rerun season yet.

Debra (23) - Another quiet year for Queen of the Party - NOT! Spent
most of her available leisure time shooting pool in the Hyatt's sports
bar. Has dated every eligible bachelor in Monterey and all adjoining
counties. Her definition of eligible: " breathing, over 5'2" and not butt
ugly". If anyone knows a young man who fits this definition and can put
up with her occasional crude and loud behavior, please contact her mother.
Steadily working her way up in the State Water Conservation community.
Future goal; politics. Has taken to wearing glasses to improve her professional image. Get this, is seriously considering changing her first
name to "Dakota". Why? Who knows probably too many frosties. Jill's
comment "go ahead as long as you also move there".

Denise (26) - She and Bryan presently hibernating in Detroit. Last year his soccer team (Detroit Rockers) successfully raced thru the playoffs to the championship. Denise was disappointed that the winner's share was not on the same level as the Redskin Super Bowl winner's share. Denise has seriously taken up golf. Recently she was talked in to entering a tournament before her game was tournament tough. Her first event was noteworthy for the following: wiffed the ball numerous times on the first tee with everyone watching, on a follow thru slipped and fell face down in a mud flat, embarassed herself by overindulging at the 19th hole. Way to go Denise; keep up the good work!!

Carol (50) - Loves those Grandmother duties especially the fact that you get to leave the little darlings with someone else when they start fussing. Celebrated her Big Fiftyth this past year with little or no bad side effects. Again competed for Fort Ord's Best Woman Golfer title and again came in second place gross. She said How Gross is 2nd Place Gross? Pretty Gross!! Promises to do better next year. With all her real estate, grandmother, and golf goings on, the Silver Castor Canadensis has been very busy this past year. Just the other day she completely undone in a moment of extreme stress, she screamed that she wished there were two of her so she could get everything done on time. I said Great, I get to sleep in the middle!

Gill (XX) - Joins the ranks of the unemployed at the end of this year. (So if any of you know of a job available whose job description reads "any moron can do this job", give me a call.) Spent a good part of the past year on the IR list with the following: 3 broken ribs (racketball injury), dislocated shoulder (basketball), ankle ligaments (tennis), acute lower back strain (clinging vine). My Shrink sayes I must act in a more dignified, grandfatherly manner during the forthcoming year.

Hope you have a very happy holiday season and the whole Goodman clan wishes you the very best for 1993....

1993

Dear Friends,

1993: What a beautiful year for the Goodman clan. Everything seemed to go right, fall directly into place, and we had nothing left to do but count our blessings.

A little general news: The year was highlighted by our 2-week trip back to the East Coast to attend my Coast Guard Academy Class 30th Reunion. Carol and I had a great time seeing many old friends (some we had not seen since 5 June 1963) and touring the Academy grounds. Since we had not been back to New London since 1973 there were many Academy changes/ new buildings to investigate. (So many, in fact, that I had trouble recognizing the old place. Either I slept through my 4 years there, my memory is failing me, or maybe a combination of both.) In addition while we were on the East Coast we visited the places where I grew up(?). Boy, have things changed in 30 years: Greenwich Village (No gays in evidence, probably all joined the military or moved to San Francisco) & Mamaroneck, New York (Checked on a old family friend's house (typical 2800 sq ft, 4 Bdr, etc) in the hood which happened to be for sale - listing price $550k and $13k/yr property taxes.. Thanks but no thanks..) All this proves you can go back if only for a visit.....

Another item: After 8 years in Monterey, Carol and I have decided it is time for a change so we bought some land and will build a house in Sequim WA (Fifteen miles from Port Angeles on the Olympic Peninsula.. Get your map out.). Intend to retire to a life of golf, fishing, racquetball and other dilettante interests. Estimate move Summer 1994..

Denise (27) - Still in Michigan while Bryan perfects his skills as the Detroit Rockers' soccer goalie. They will probably be returning to California next year. Denise is finishing up studies at Eastern Michigan University; getting a teaching certificate and possibly a master degree. Her goal is to teach at the high school level. This from a woman who played hookey during her entire 9 grade in Hawaii to go surfing. When questioned about this her response was "I can handle it I know all the tricks".

Debra (24) - Still single and intends to remain that way indefinitely. Says she can't find a man who makes a good living, can cook/clean, and take care of the kids. When questioned about children she quickly repeats that old WC Field's line: How do I like kids? Two minutes on each side. By October had dated all the eligible bachelors in Monterey County between the ages of 16 and 36. In November she moved to Sacramento to begin a new job with the US Department of Interior, Bureau of Reclamation (?). Her official title is Water Resource Management Specialist (GS-11/12).

Jill (22) - Bartender at Monterey Hyatt Hotel's sports bar. Now if I can only convince another relative to be the starter at Pebble Beach Golf Course. She has made a commitment to clean up her language less her 1-year old daughter, Gabriella, picks up the spicy talk.. (Carol should have paid more attention to her language when our kids were growing up. I personally never did much cursing.) Gabriella, or Gaby as she is known, is California's youngest Jenny Craig signup. In addition Gaby daily opens her first book more than her mother opened any of her books in her 4-year high school career. Although somewhat biased, Carol is of the opinion that Gaby is the brightest, prettiest, cutest, most coordinated baby in the entire Universe. (Oh Lord, spare me from new Grandmothers in heat.)

Carol (X) - Mature Magazine's 1993 Junior Grandmother of the Year.. Golf/ fishing on the back burner.. Spent considerable time designing the new Sequim house. During the final design review the contractor noted no kitchen was included. When questioned her reply was "Screw it, I intend to eat out every day". What about resale value? A house must have a kitchen. She reconsidered and her design was approved.

Gill (X+1) - Tough life which someone must endure. What with golf, fishing, racquetball not much time left to read USA Today's sports section or the Wall Street Journal. Total elasped time since employment/work - 1 year and counting.. (Many would argue that during most of his Coast Guard career, although employed, he was essentially "workfree".) Presently job hunting in earnest: maximum time expended each week - 10 minutes.

May-Ling Too (3) - Sharp teeth. Exceptional sniffer. Fast Runner. Best friend to all family members.

Hope you have a very happy holiday season and the whole Goodman clan wishes you the best for 1994......

Gill & Carol

1994

19 December 1994

Dear Friends,

As I enter the autumn of my years or at least the late, late summer, I have decided on shorter letters. So here goes for 1994. First of all, Carol and I are still in Monterey waiting for our condo to sell. As soon as it does, off to Sequim, Washington we will go. Our land up north now has a well dug, foundation in, building permit approved and that's as far as we will go until a Monterey sale is pending. But no problem, during the wait Carol and I are enjoying working out at the health club, messing up on the golf course, and watching Oprah. With those opening remarks recorded for all the ages, here is some Goodman news:

Denise (28) - Bryan signed a new 3-year contract with the Detroit Rockers' soccer team. Good bucks, secure job, what the heck, they might be in Michigan until 2000. Denise recently received her teaching certificate and will assume the duties of a high school English class warden very soon.

Debra (25) - Water Resource Management Specialist (Sounds like a fancy title for a plumber, doesn't it?). Still working diligently in Sacramento for the US Bureau of Reclamation. Single and will stay that way for a while. Soon to be the sole VIP guest on Ricki Lake's 300th anniversary show (you guess the subject); watch for her.

Jill (23) - Executive Assistant for Monterey's Hyatt General Manager and loves her job. Very busy taking care of her 2-year old daughter, Gabriella. Gaby is a precocious 2-year old presently taking postgraduate courses at our local Montessori school. Reminds everyone of Debra with some common sense.

May-Ling II (4) - World's smartest Shih Tzu. Gaby's best friend.

Carol (X) - Enjoying grandmotherhood, exercise, and golf. Looking forward to her sister's (Sharon) upcoming wedding here in Monterey.

Gill (X+1) - No problems, no problems.. Although presently on the IR with a dislocated right shoulder, should be back playing right-handed racquetball by the Super Bowl. Golf handicap rising, sexual activity declining, hair falling, and afternoon naps a must. Oh, the beauty of it all...

Hope you all have a very happy holiday season and we wish you the best for 1995....

Gill & Carol

1995

15 December 1995

Dear Friends,

As much as I hate to say it, I cound probably just xerox last year's
letter, stuff it in an envelope, and mail it since nothing really earth
shattering has happened since the last letter. Carol and I are still in
Monterey waiting for our condo to sell so we can complete our move to
Sequim, Washington. (Our Sequim lot has a house foundation and well and
sits patiently awaiting the "Build It" command.) While we wait, we continue to enjoy the Monterey scene as a couple of retired, middle age AARP
members; lots of golf, afternoon naps, exercising to keep the body young,
watching a granddaughter grow, and enjoying fishing during the best Monterey salmon season in the past 20 years. Vacations during 1995 included:
Las Vegas to participate in a golf tournament (finally won at tables),
Sequim twice to visit with DJ Aites and Den/Bev Bluett, and Southern California for the tenth annual Goodman Open golf Tournament (great to see
the old crowd; Culbertsons, Lees, Taylors et al). Okay now some 1995 news:

Denise (29) - Still located in a Detroit suburb. Denise teaching at a
local high school. Bryan continues as goalie for the Detroit Rockers'
soccer team and conducts numerous off season soccer camps. (Good bucks and
secure jobs. Great !!) Both are actively involved remodeling/decorating
their first house which is located on a lake.

Debra (26) - Continues as a Water Resource Management Specialist for the
US Bureau of Reclamation in Sacramento. Still single and proud of having
terrorized almost all the eligible male YUPPIES in central California.
Intends to return to college in 1996 and get her MPA degree (Lucky
university and method of financing still to be determined.).

Jill (24)   - Customer Relations Specialist for Cellular One in Monterey.
Loves the job since the majority of her time is spent on the telephone
talking with someone else picking up the phone bill. (An extension of her
teenage years! If this keeps up someday she'll have to have the telephone
surgerically remove from her right ear.) Gaby, her precocious 3-year old,
was recently brought up on charges of extorting little boys' lunches at
the local Montessori school.

May-Ling II (5) - World's best Shih Tzu. Gaby's best friend.

Carol (X) - The Silver Castor Canadensis spent the year enjoying grandmotherhood, exercise, and golf(14). After years of second place finishes
finally became Fort Ord's woman golf champion. (Came from 2 down with 3
to play to win going away..) Attributes this success to her exercise
program, wine before dinner, and her new health diet (see below).

Gill (X+1) - Still playing golf(6), racquetball, and fishing. Some consulting work but not enough to be considered "employed" under the Clinton/
Panetta guidelines. Now does all the cooking for the family. (No more
haole food. Everything is spicy hot. Jambalaya and tacos for Thanksgiving. Yes!! Life is good. The real secret of Carol's golfing successes..
Remember if you don't feel it moving around all night in your stomach, it
ain't hot enough.)

Hope you all have a very happy holiday season and we wish you the best for
1996....

Gill & Carol

1996

18 December 1996

Dear Friends,

Still in Monterey waiting for a "big bucks" buyer for our condo. Nothing yet but we are hoping for a spring sale. Only news about our Sequim lot is that we got the septic system in before the permit expired. We now have an acre with a house foundation, well, the new septic system and that's all. (Carol intends to personally break in the new septic system during next summer's visit. For the past 2 months she has been diligently practicing using the "hover" technique over an open 4 inch pipe.) Now for all the news that is fit to print:

Denise (29.87) - Professor Emeritus at a suburban Detroit high school; teaching 9th grade. (Must be rather difficult since she has no personal 9th grade experience to fall back on. Spent that entire year "playing the hook" from her Hawaiian high school while learning to surf and drag race. Bet she can't say to her students "When I was in 9th grade ...." without cracking a smile.) During the past year Bryan and her spent most of their leisure time landscaping their lake front house. Used an Army surplus flamethrower to thaw the ground for the late fall bulb planting.

Debra (27) - Attending Syracuse University's Maxwell School in search of a MPA degree or a Mrs. designation whichever comes first. From the looks of things the degree seems more likely. (Graduation next June.) Spent last month interviewing for her next job. Most promising so far is a consulting firm in Houston. Isn't sure what to think... Says a cowboy hat & boots do nothing for her; unless of course that's all he is wearing. Voted by her student peers as "Oldest, Loudest, and Horniest Bachelor-ette". Nice, Deb, very nice!!! That will be the subject of lots of laughs and discussion at class reunions 20 years down the road.

Jill (25) - Job promotion. Is now Corporate Client Specialist (?) for Cellular One in Monterey/Salinas. Queen of the Soap Operas. She doesn't watch them she lives them. A crisis here, a crisis there, a crisis everywhere! And now a new serious romance? An engagement ring? Stay tuned for flash announcements or next year's letter..... Gaby, her almost perfect 4-year old, attended this year's Little Indian Princesses Halloween Party as Queen Running Mouth. Perfect, this kid talks more than Rush Limbaugh

May-Ling II (6) - World's best Shih Tzu. Has more brains and a higher IQ than half the family (that is Carol's half of course).

Carol (X) - Poster child for California's 1996 Cure Mageiricophobia* Campaign. The Silver Castor Canadensis spent another year enjoying grandmotherhood, exercise, and golf(12). Used her trusty 3-wood to ace Fort Ord's 6th Hole, a 155-yard monster. Continues to retell all the crappy details of this lucky shot to anyone who will listen. Boring. Carol, no one cares about it once its over. When Fort Ord's Men's (?)

Golf Team was short a man, she volunteered to fill the breech and play from the white tees in the big playoff match. As the attached newspaper clipping attests won her first match against some embarrassed male who was heard commenting in the bar afterwards "They shouldn't allow women within 10 miles of the front gate of a golf course.". She was brought back to earth the following week when her Monterey Peninsula Country Club opponent was a 6'4" transvestite in drag who could hit the ball further than Tiger. So there Carol.

Gill (X+1) - Averaging 200+/year for past 4 years. Guys get that amazed expression off your faces we're talking about rounds of golf here. Handicap (4) continues to go down. Is there no limit? Regretably I'll bet there is. Known around Monterey County as The King of Creative Combing.. Hates that title; as a military man prefers to consider it Strategic Deployment of Available Resources. In either case dome is getting tougher to cover each year. As Carol says "Dear, your fivehead is showing again." Enough, enough and no I don't want to hear about that damm golf shot again.

* Mageiricophobia is the intense fear of having to cook.

BIRDIES & BOGEYS
Bob Hughes

Fort Ord's team competing in the NCGA's Thursday competition brought in a ringer in last week's match against Pajaro Valley at Bayonet. Carol Goodman, a diminutive sweet swinger with the competitive stare of Dottie Pepper and the fluid putting stroke of Ben Crenshaw, captured her match over an embarrassed nameless male. It wasn't a suprise to husband Gil or team captain Dick Dahlinger, who had scouted Carol before signing her.

THE MONTEREY COUNTY HERALD
MONDAY, SEPTEMBER 23, 1996

Sports

Hope you all have a very happy holiday season and we wish you the best for 1997....

Carol & Gill

1997

15 December 1997

Dear Friends,

After waiting three plus years for the Monterey condo to sell, the blessed event happened in February and we had 21 days to vacate quarters. No problem; using Coast Guard training/experience we were gone within the alloted time frame. Construction of our new Sequim houses started in April and we moved in 1 July. The reason I say houses was that a small outbuilding, originally designed for Carol to practice her craft crap, grew into a full-fledged guest house. (Stop laughing, you guys. I got sucked in. It happens occasionally even to the most street smart.) So we are now permanently residing in Sequim and Retirement Phase II has been initiated. Joined a great little "Q-Tip" country club with lots of golf tournaments and active senior members. Weather has been wonderful (so far El Nino has pushed all the winter stuff to California) and the scenery is amazing. Now for all the true stories that are fit to print:

Denise (30) - Still Professor Emeritus at a suburban Detroit high school; teaching 11/12th grade. Highlight of year was active partici- pation in two woman's wrestling events on the same night in two of suburban Detroit's finest watering holes. Seems Denise and a few of her closest girlfriends decided to celebrate her 30th birthday at a quiet restaurant for dinner and a few beers. One of her girlfriends (5'2", 100lbs) got into an altercation with a rather large female at the next barstool. Denise stepped in because of the obvious size inequality and the next thing you know an all female barroom brawl. After the police came and threw everyone out, Denise and her crowd went 5 miles across town to another establishment to continue with dinner. Damm if they don't run into the same Amazon and her gang and guess what? Round 2! The police released Denise to husband Bryan if he promised to take Rocky home. Denise, protector of the downtrodden/underdog, you certainly know how to make an old sailor proud. Building memories.

Debra (28) - Graduated from Syracuse University's Maxwell School with a MPA degree in July. Accepted a management consultant with Deloitte & Touche (one of the big five[?]) with her home base back in Sacramento. Has spent the last three months working on a major consulting project in Pasadena and coming home every weekend. Believes her 70+ hour workweeks are duty above and beyond. Sayes in her next life wants to be like her Father; a Coast Guard Captain with 20-hour workweeks. (I never got around to telling her about that year loran duty on a frozen, isolated Alaskan island or those wonderful months on ocean station floating in the North Atlantic off Greenland in the winter, etc.)

Jill (26) - Still a Corporate Client Coordinator for Cellular One in Monterey/Salinas. Remains queen of the soap operas. A crisis here, a crisis there, a crisis everywhere! Still single for the time being. Gabriella, her almost perfect, precocious 5-year old, appears to have atleast 7 or 8 years until the brain dead teenage years arrive. But even now dreaded teenage characteristics are starting to emerge. Spent a month with us in Sequim this summer at the conclusion of which we volunteered to drive her home to Monterey. After about five hours on the road went ballistic during a power struggle with Grandpa over her portable radio volume level. When she stopped screaming and crying was heard to mutter "I'm not having a good day. I wish I'd never been born." Where have I heard that before? Recently watching her mother get into those thong (butt floss) skivees Jill favors, she informed her mother that they should go shopping for new underwear that would properly "cover your fat butt. You know, the big, baggy kind Grandma wears".

May-Ling II (7) - World's best Shih Tzu. Loves new house. Patrols the acreage perimeter like a true watchdog.

Carol (X) - The Silver Castor Canadensis is enjoying grandmotherhood, landscaping, and golf(12). Handled the move with determination, perseverence, and skill. Towing our 22-foot boat (7000 lbs) behind our newly acquired Ford F250 truck from Monterey to Sequim was a 3-day ordeal. Of the 22 actual on the road hours, Carol drove 20. (As you all well know I get alittle nervous during stressful conditions. Anyways, I was a good navigator.) The highlight to this trip was her handling of the rig when the trailer's wheel bearings failed coming down the north side of Oregon's Siskiyou Mountains. When she finally got the rig stopped it took them 3 hours to get me off the seat due to the rosettes I had pulled on the way down. She is now respectfully known up and down Interstate 5 as "Grand Mother Trucker" or something like that.

Gill (X+1) - Golf(5), racquetball, fishing, and landscaping. Yes landscaping!! I do the butt work (e,g., dig holes, wheelbarrow manure, etc.) and Carol gets to go around trimming the trees and poseys. Near as I can figure by next summer the entire 1.2 acres will be "landscaped" and I'll be broke and exhausted. A little good news to report... Although only a few family member knew I have been battling a very serious medical condition for the past 10 years. With the help of some wonderful doctors, both here in Seattle and San Francisco, and the latest in miracle drug therapy, extensive tests conducted during last month's annual physical clearly indicated that my long battle with ephebiphobia has been won. No residual physical or mental effects were evident. Doctors say I have probably 7 or 8 years until the condition reappears. I intend to fully enjoy whatever time I have left.

Hope you all have a wonderful holiday season and very successful 1998.

Best Wishes,

CAROL & GILL
The Goodmans

Ephebiphobia = loathing (fear) of teenagers

1998

5 December 1998

Dear Friends,

Its been another good year for all of us, but before giving highlights
I must relate a recent conversation and then set the record straight!
I was gossiping with a friend when she said how much her twenty something daughter loved my Christmas letter but could not believe how I
could make up those stories about my family members and then air the
dirty linen for all the world to see. First, let me assure all of
you, I have never made up stuff about my family members. They are only
too happy to provide unbelievably bizarre, actual experiences to make
this letter easier to write. Secondly, each and every family member
reads the letter and has final authority to delete any and all items
they find offensive before mailing. In the 16 years I have written
the Christmas letter only one deletion request has been received and
acted upon. It was last year and concerned daughter Debra's torrid,
tawdry 4-month affair with Adam Sandler (The Waterboy). [Or was it
Macauly Caukins (Home Alone) I can never remember which one since she
had a fling with both.] In any case, when things got serious and the
actor(?) wouldn't sign the prenuptial, she broke it off. Debra's law-
yers requested that I remove the item from the Christmas letter at
least until the actor's Alienation of Affection lawsuit was settled.

All events in 1998 were overshadowed by the addition of another beautiful, bright, and healthy granddaughter. Jill gave birth to Sophia
Marie in Monterey on 15 October. Welcome aboard!! Yes, another
female, making the grand total of Goodman squatters lots. Brings to
mind that old CGHQ battle cry when another touchy feely administration
edict was promulgated "Damm, doesn't anyone have any stones around
here?" In my family's case, regrettably the answer is no.

During the past year two vacations stand out in my mind as real fun
times:
    1. Infamous Goodman Open 1998 Version - Held at the Sudden
Valley Golf & CC; Belllingham, WA with General Manager Chic Murray
(CGA-64) in command. We had a great time playing golf and visiting
with old friends. But I still have reoccurring nightmares on how to
play the impossible #9 hole. (Note: The 14th annual Goodman Open will
be held in Sequim on 4-7 August 1999. Make your reservations early!)
    2. Fishing Trip to Bamfield, British Columbia - Carol, Brian,
Denise, and I took the family boat (22' Grady White) 80 miles NNW to
Barkley Sound on the west coast of Vancouver Island (i.e., out into
the Pacific). We caught plenty salmon and halibut but even more fun
was the boat trip up and back. Just like GITMO: We set the Special
Sea Detail, exercised the Fog Navigation Team, utilized CIC plotting
techniques, initiated damage control drills, and I even held Captain's
Mast (Article 15) once. (On one bouncy morning Carol came unglued and
was downright insubordinate. Brian booked her. At Mast she received 2
days restriction to her bunk. And at the end of those 2 days I can
still honestly say "I never had sexual relations with THAT woman.")

Denise (30+) - Husband Brian and her still residing in suburban
Detroit. Quiet year for Denise; not even a parking ticket to spoil
her 1998 record. (Recently her Parole Officer voted her Most Likely
to Succeed as her 18-month parole term expired. Well done, Denise!)
She is now teaching in junior high school and once her students
learned of her record she has had very little disruption/trouble in
her classroom. In her spare time finishing her work toward a Masters
Degree in Education. Who would have thought...

Debra (29) - Still employed as a management consultant with the famous firm of Deloitte & Touche. Recently promoted to Senior Management
Consultant, making her one of the head Touches. Congratulations!
Another round of vinegar and water for the everyone. Although still
home based in Sacramento spent considerable time working in Pasadena
and Oklahoma City. Says next spring she will be working in Helena,
Montana for a few months. Great choices!! {Debra, how high up the
corporate ladder do you have to be to get a few months in Hawaii or
Barcelona? Is there a glass ceiling involved? Remind them you are
now a head Touches. And one last point if you do ever get on the
other side of the glass ceiling, remember to wear slacks or at least
underpants if you wear a skirt.}

Jill (27) - Remains a Corporate Client Coordinator for Cellular One
in Salinas. In constant motion with two daughters, but appears that
she is winning the war and most of the battles. Gabriella, her precocious 6-year old, graduated as Valedictorian from her Kindergarden
last spring and received a full academic scholarship to Public School
#35 (according to her grandmother).

May-Ling II (8) - Voted Best of Breed at Sequim's 75th Annual Dog
Show. Doesn't matter that she is the only Shih Tzu with papers on the
Olympic Peninsula.

C. Goodman (X-1) - What are the odds of one grandmother having the
world's two most perfect grandchildren? But listening to her it has
happened. (Pray spare us the pictures this time, lady.) The Silver
Castor Canadensis plays alot of golf(10), landscapes, works in her
garden, does arts and crafts leaving little time to supervise/cor-
rect/service husband. Loves living in Sequim!

Gill (X) - Golf(4), racquetball, and fishing. Also loves living in
Sequim. A quiet year for a quiet guy(?). Looking forward to next
summer's boat trip/fishing adventure to Alaska. Now spends hours
rolling small steel balls around in his hand.

Hope you all have a wonderful holiday season and very successful 1999.

                    Best Wishes,
                    Gil & Carol
                    The Goodmans

1999

28 December 1999

Dear Friends,

I started this Christmas letter the day after Thanksgiving and I am still trying to get it out. In previous years I would compose/type the silly thing on my IBM XT (vintage 1982) computer in 3 hours max. But now because Carol had to have a new, hot s.... computer with Windows 98, + + + + , a scanner and all the bells and whistles. It has taking me a month to figure out how to use this "simple" word processor. Progress - one step forward two steps back for us old folks. Alright just bear with me and I'll get this ship written. righted.

Another year goes by and small things happen. Nothing big, nothing bad; which is good just the way I like it. No surprises, everything planned and executed according to the approved plan of attack. I love to say those things because they p.... Carol off. She says don't you ever do anything on the spur of the moment? I tell her "Yea once I had flatulence." That makes her even madder. Don't you just love it! Now that I've got you in the proper frame of mind for my Christmas letter, lets give it a try.

Highlight of 1999 was Jill getting married to Jerry Esquivel in April. Their wedding, held in Monterey, CA, ranked right up there with Denise's quiet little fiasco 8 years ago in Dana Point. (That one, if you can remember, was the last time, prior to the Seattle/WTO event, that martial law was declared and the National Guard was called in to quiet a civil disturbance. I still have recurring nightmares.) In any case, welcome aboard to Jerry, the hard working and prosperous landowner/farmer in both the Salinas Valley and Yuma, AZ. He is a great addition to our tribe. Now only one left- If anyone out there in readerland knows of any breathing male with an IQ over 30 that Debra hasn't already dated, we would appreciate it if you forward his name and signed medical release for Debra's review. (She is looking for a tall, rich, dumb, house husband-type she can brow beat into submission.)

Best vacation of 1999 was another trip in our boat up the west coast of Vancouver Island to a place called Bamfield in Barkley Sound. Eleven days of great salmon/halibut fishing and beautiful scenery. So good in fact that we are going to do it again for two weeks or so next August.

Now for a few tidbits and news about tribe members:

Denise (30++) - Still living in the Detroit area with long suffering husband Bryan. (Honest Denise, he asked me to include the adjectives.) Last year taught in a local high school and this year in a junior high. I assumed her demotion (?) was due to the fact that the authorities had finally gotten their hands on a copy of Denise's own high school attendance records and resulting truancy convictions. But no, she assures me that her reassignment to this tough, "blackboard jungle" junior high school was a direct result of the administration learning of her world class pugilist talents and record. After a year of junior high she swears next year she will be teaching pre-kindergarden in an all girls Catholic school..

Debra (30) - Still employed as a Senior Management Consultant with Deloitte Consulting, Inc. in Sacramento. (Formally Deloitte &Touche but they split. No more Touche. There goes 30% of my joke material.) Debra's a strange woman- Owns two cars (one brand new, one a few years old) so she will always have one running while the other is in the shop for repairs from her fender benders. She refers to this concept as her Universal Unit Replacement Program and intends to implement it for boyfriends in 2000. This should ensure a replacement male companion available immediately if she physical damages the incumbent. This from an honors graduate of UCSB and Syracuse's esteemed Maxwell School of Management. Debbie, strongly suggest keeping a lower profile or they are going to ask for their degrees back. As noted before still single and actively in the hunt.

Jill (28) · Now a stay-at-home mother of two; Gabriella (7) and Sophia (1). Lord, you should hear her crybaby about how tough parenting is and why don't her kids listen and obey. HA. Just wait: Little kids little problems, big kids big problems. The fun is just beginning and I get to watch instead of participating this time. I can't wait!! Now I know why grandparents and grandkids get along so great: They have a common enemy.

May-Ling II (9) · Best dog in the world. As Carol said the other day as I carried May Ling out to pee (it had rained, the lawn was wet); "You treat that dog better than you did your kids!" Of course, this little dear never pokes fun at her father, never back talks, never argues, etc... (By the way she is in my will for an equal share with the rest of the tribe and she knows it - I told her so the other day in doggie talk.)

Carol (X-1) · Won the 1999 Women's Golf Championship at our local country club. Her picture now hangs in a place of distinction in the club's entrance way and she is known throughout the community as "The Champ". Earlier this year she finally quit smoking and is looking healthy again. The Silver Castor Canadensis is so healthy, in fact, that she is up two weight classes and now a top contender in the WBA's welterweight division. Once again voted Top Grandmother in the Sequim area at the annual contest attended by thousands on Grandparent's Day. Contest consisted of who could induce sleep in all 5 judges the quickest by the telling anecdote, showing pictures etc., etc. of the precious grandchildren. Carol won hands down. (It is interesting to watch Carol out in the public (e.g., Costco, main street, Town Tavern, etc.) people avoid her like the plague; they can't take another 5 minutes listening about the adorable little ones.) Working hard at her hobbies: gardening, stain glass, candle making, Victoria Secret modeling (mature division), etc., etc...

Gill (X) · Lost the 1999 Men's Golf Championship at our local country club by one shot after incurring a 2-stroke penalty for an improper drop. My picture now hangs in the men's room (third stall from the left) and I am known, unfortunately, throughout the community as "The Chump". (This is true: We have received mail addressed to "Champ and Chump Goodman". Some individuals just have to put people down to make themselves appear better. Being a FOB I hope he can feel my pain.) In the Spring I will be leaving for two months TAD in the New York City area. Because I speak the language fluently and have extensive knowledge of the local culture (?), I have been hired as a senior advance man for Hillary's forthcoming senatorial campaign. I can't think of a better, more honest or deserving candidate to rally behind. (If you believe that last TAD tidbit or my BS comment about her candidacy, I have a bridge I want to sell you.)

I would like to end this letter with a beauty from W.C. Fields "A Merry Christmas to all my friends except two." But Carol says I can't, so let me end it with:

Hope you all had a wonderful holiday season and a very successful 2000!!!!

Best Wishes,
The Goodmans

2000

1 December 2000

Dear Friends,

Early Christmas letter this year. Finally got organized and caught up. Wonderful feeling!!! No big problems this past year. Everything dead solid perfect straight down the middle.

The biggest news this year is the forthcoming birth of three new grandchildren; Jill later this month and Denise twins in February. Now for the real amazing news, medical science has determined that all will be male offspring. The first in our family in the last two generations. No more Barbies or Easy Bake ovens - footballs and manly things will be in vogue.. A true miracle!!! It should be the most joyful of times for all concerned, what with new life coming and especially news of the very long awaited boy babies. But alas that is not the case. Things have gotten very tense. We have reached a point where nobody is even talking to one another. It is sister against sister with even their mother involved. I, of all people, should have fore-seen the potential problem and taken steps to alleviate it but I blew it. It all started with a telephone call to me from Jill where she said "You are the greatest and I hold you in such high esteem I intend to name my first son Gill." I, of course, said yes - Good idea!!!. Denise called the next day and unaware of Jill's tele-phone call said essentially the same thing except she wanted to name both of the twins Gill. (Sort of like George Foremen's four sons George,....,...., and George). An amazing tribute and one I'm not sure I am worthy. But probably yes.. About a week later when one sister after another proudly informed their mother that her grandson(s) would be Baby Gill all hell broke loose. Serious name calling between sisters ensued followed by comments such as: I had the name first., I've known him longer., I was always his favorite.. It was so sweet.. It brought back memories of when they were all teenagers. After considerable reflection I had the perfect solution: the first boy should be Gill, the second Gil, and the third Gilly. What could bring more happiness at future family gatherings then Grandpa Gill surrounded by a flock of little Gillys? The thought brings a warm feeling to the heart and a tear to the eye.. Carol says forgitaboutit! More>>

Denise (30+++) - Still residing in the Detroit area although husband Brian is now playing for the Buffalo soccer team. Denise's teaching career has been put on hold as she awaits the birth of Baby Gill x 2. Since we are known worldwide as Parents Extraordinary, Denise has come to Carol and I many times to discuss how to best handle her forthcoming parenthood. I have spent considerable time giving her my valuable parenting secrets: join the Coast Guard, go on many electronics TAD trips, volunteer for extended shipboard duty, and don't come home until all offspring are at least 20 years old. Pay attention, Denise! Remember Carol and I were voted Parents of the Year (1972) at the Cape May officer's club bar althought a hand recount of the ballots is still being conducted.

Debra (30+) - Presently in between jobs residing in the Sacramento area. Decided that working continuous 70++ hour weeks was not only infringing on her social life but should be outlawed as a public health issue. Intends to get reemployed after the holiday season.

Jill (29) - With husband Jerry (the hardworking gentleman landowner/farmer) and crew recently moved into their new, big home just north of Salinas. Jill now a stay-at-home mother of Gabriella (8), Sophia (2), and Baby Gill (-1 month) is busy, busy busy. Her days are highlighted by such noteworthy events as yesterday's monumental, long-awaited announcement that "Baby Phia (as she refers to herself) finally put one in the toilet and diapers will be gone soon". Just reaffirms my belief that a good life is defined as a string of small successes one after another that usually comes full circle as one gets older. Pretty profound, eh? Jill, be advised, I will be particularly upset if during my next visit Baby Gill tells me his two older sisters are verbally harassing him. Remember, Jill, all you Goodman women are carriers of your mother's aggressive XMEAN gene.

May-Ling II (10) - "Doggie Emeritus".

Carol (old) - Golf, gardening, stained glass, a quintessential jack of all crafts. A Martha Sewart clone.. Must relate an interesting episode that occurred recently: Carol received for Mother's Day a remote controlled, battery powered golf cart that transports her clubs around the course while the Silver Castor Canadensis in command walks a short distance behind. It is powered by a VDC battery just slightly smaller than a car battery. To allow her to charge one while the other is in use she has two identical batteries. When I installed the battery charger in the garage I noticed that it was possible, if one wasn't careful, to mistake the spare battery connection for the charger cable connector and connect batteries directly to each other resulting in a massive discharge. I warned Carol and even showed her how it was possible to make this "rookie mistake". It wasn't 2 weeks later that Carol came stumbling into the kitchen using very bad language (note to self: teach her how to pronounce the f word properly). Her hands were black, complexion very red, and her hair had the same pin curl design as little orphan Annie. All in all, she looked like Debra at age 2 just after the kid stuck a safety pin into the 120 VAC wall socket. I immediately noted she probably had no permanent physiological damage and based on the widely successful Coast Guard training mantra "Teach while the issue is hot"; I proceeded to try to instill in Carol a comprehensive understanding of God's golden rule: E = IR. I explained voltage potential difference, zero resistance hence large current flow. At the conclusion of the lecture if I had had a group of engineering students without doubt they would have gotten up in unison and rendered me a standing ovation such was my dramatic and detailed engineering explanation. Carol instead used the f word several times (Again terribly mispronounced but this time at least accompanied by the appropriate one-finger salute.) Carol started talking to me again in about a month. Strange woman!!. Either they want to be enlightened or they don't!

Gill (older) - Golf (3), racquetball, and fishing.. What else is there in a perfect life!! Did have one rather interesting event occur during the past year. About a two months after Carol tried to electrocute herself (see above) I noticed that the GFI receptacle in the garage kept tripping. Using F,D &I (i.e., fault, detection and isolation) techniques and procedures honed to a razor's edge during my 35-year electronics career I set about finding and correcting the problem. After about an hour into the corrective maintenance effort, you guessed it, I shorted Carol's aforementioned VDC batteries together permanently as the amazing discharge effectively welded everything into one big molten mess. Picture this: a beautiful combover now standing straight up. Photos taken by the USAA accident investigation team show me looking like a one sided, honky Don King with charred hands. When Carol returned from a shopping trip hours later my cover story was faulty ground in the charger caused the fire. (Actual cause of the original GFI problem defective second hand freezer.) I now stay pretty much in front of the television and call the repairman when something is amiss.

I hated high school French but my stepmother (bless her soul) said "Stop whining because you'll use it when you get older.". Well I never have till now, but here goes - Let me leave you with one of the only two things I learned in that class (I hope I get the pronunciation right.) : Laissez le bon temps roullez!! What is the other thing I learned? You'll have to wait until next year. Till then --

Hope all your putts are center cut, you all have a wonderful holiday season and a very successful 2001.

Best Wishes,
The Goodmans

2001

Dear Friends,

This year's Christmas letter will take a slightly different form this year: some serious words, a true (hopefully humorous) story , a few facts and observations, and a closing. Although the Goodman clan continues smoothly along with peaks and valleys, everyone's world was spun around on 9/11/01. Permit me a few words on NYC's tragedy: I grew up about a mile from "ground zero" and did not move out to the Westchester's suburbs until my parents realized that unless they relocated the only college that I would be eligible for would be Wiseguy U. Although I finally left NY in 1959 and except for a day here and there on vacation never returned, I, by nature, temperament, and accent, remain a New Yorker. The events of 9-11 have left me sad and pretty mad!! A tragedy caused by a demented few. My wish for 2002 is that a good start be made in ridding the world of (or safely containing) all terrorists and zealots regardless of race, religion, national origin or whatever. "We must accept finite disappointment, but we must never lose infinite hope." - (ML King Jr.)

That said let me continue this year's letter with (I swear) a true story: Carol and I spent last Christmas season and on into January with Jerry, Jill, and grandkids in Salinas, CA. Near the end of that period one of the strangest happenings in my lifetime occurred: It started with the unheralded NY football Giants ending up in the Super Bowl. As the days before the big game dwindled down I, the biggest Giant fan of all, was beyond myself mouthing off everywhere. I loaded up bets with my bookie and settled on a plan of attack for the big day. Our plan was that Joe Splane (my old buddy), middle daughter Debbie, and I would visit a few local sports bars to prelube (and bother 49er fans) and then return to Jill's to watch the game. On game day our execution was perfect as I was in my seat all properly beered up at kick off . By halftime the handwriting was on the wall, that is, the Giants were getting mauled/dead. I could not stand the intense pain and switched to tequila shooters with beer backs. At the end of the third quarter I was horizontal on the couch almost comatose. I never did see the end of the game because I had layed down on my bed just to rest my eyes.   At about 2 am I awoke noting that the tequila/beer was winning (and maybe a head cold coming on) and I desperately needed medicine. In a dark kitchen, in a strange house, I found the little cardboard rectangle with the tylenol tablets. I took three of them and staggered back to bed and I quickly fell back to sleep which was interrupted by a warm, fuzzy dream - I was on the Oprah show. I mean I "was on" the Oprah show!! I was in a female body and could hear my voice talking to Dr. Phil about my issues (low self esteem, monthly depression, etc.). The all-female audience was to a woman sympathetic with tears forming in the corner of every eye. Wow - I woke up quick. That was too weird!! My head hurt even worse, the tequila/ beer/cold was winning again so back to the dark kitchen for four more Tylenol. Again to sleep for an hour or two. This time I woke up drenched in perspiration with the heat rushing from my stomach area toward my head - damn I was having a quintessential female hot flash. Wow, that was really too weird!! Got my clothes on and staggered back to the kitchen where Carol saw me . Her comment was "You look terrible. Have you taken any medicine?" I said "Yes, seven or so Tylenol". She said show me what you took since we have been out of Tylenol for the past three days. The mini investigation revealed I had taken multiple doses of Estroven ("Naturally helps support hormonal balance during menopause."). The ER doctor on duty at Monterey hospital recommended that I check my package at least twice a day and asked if I had experienced any recent breast development. Funny guy!!

Denise (30+++) -   Still residing in the Detroit area with husband Brian and now twins; Joshua and Owen. As the grandmother and mother describe the twins - They are the most beautiful, smartest, best behaved, ...,... , etc. twins in the history of twindom.

Debra (30+) - Still in the Sacramento area working as a consultant trying to straighten out and stream-line California's welfare system. That project has the potential for a lifetime of future employment.

Jill (29) - Safely settled down in her new house (Salinas foothills) with husband Jerry, daughters Gabby(9) and Sophia(3) and Joseph (aka Little Gilly). The prototypical young mother running here, there and everywhere. A short comment regarding granddaughter Sophia: This kid has all the right stuff (i.e., super intelligent, listens to no one, attitude/a mean streak, rebellious, speaks her mind, curses like a sailor) to provide great material for the next 20 or so Christmas letters. May no one correct or discipline this child in any manner that could possibly damage her God-given negative creativity.

May-Ling II (11) - "Super Doggie Emeritus". My best friend. I'm firmly convinced that the old adage "All dogs go to heaven" is true, at least for Shih Tzus.

Carol (old) - Golf (11), gardening, stained glass, a jack of all crafts. The Silver Castor Canadensis spent the past year travelling to be there for the birth of all grandsons and then revisisting later in the year to ensure the little boys were being properly cared for. Sort of like an in-family social worker/inspector.

Gill (60) - Golf (4), racquetball, and fishing.. Another almost perfect year until mid-summer when I began to feel a strange twinge in my left shoulder at the top of my classic golf swing follow thru. Finally at one of my weekly golf lessons Butch Harmon said "Hell, even the 80-year old woman members are out hitting you now - get medical help." Last week the surgeon fixed a completely torn rotator cuff, busted ligament, a small bone spur. The surgeon guaranteed me that if I faithfully rehab I would be ready when my Master's invitation arrives next year.

A short footnote: This will be the last year for this type cutesy Christmas letter. Some of you will miss it, I guess, others will say good. I think the time has come, maybe overdue. What form future Goodman Christmas letters(?) will take is anyone's guess; maybe another family member will take pen in hand , maybe I'll want to get back in the saddle after a reasonable sabbatical, in any case rest assured that in the future, like this year, you will be in our prayers and always have our best wishes for all health and happiness.

Hope all your drives are in the fairway or at least the short rough.. You all have a wonderful holiday season and a very successful 2002.

Best Wishes,
The Goodmans

2002

December 15, 2002

Merry Christmas and a Happy, Healthy New Year!!!!

I am sorry to report that our head writer has retired. I thought he was just babbling last year when he said that was his last Goodman Clan update. You are stuck with the second in command and I will attempt to fill you in. I would just send cards but I have always felt that a little update about family and lifestyle was required to really keep in touch. I can see the future, I just received my first Christmas card via email. Not a bad idea.

Gill: 60+ Cranky! Plays racquetball three times a week, golf four times a week and a couch potato on NFL Sundays. He is gearing up for a visit this Christmas with the grandchildren and their parents. (Parents are required to accompany all children.) Says he will write next year's Christmas letter if he is allowed to use the anecdote regarding my recent annual physical. I say NO WAY.

Carol: 60 Gardener, crafter, golfer. Enjoys being a grandparent. Church volunteer. Have witnessed the curse/blessing I put on my children (i.e., they will have children just like them). Debra says she may not have children after she visits her nieces and nephews. She says it is way too much work.

Denise, Bryan, Joshua & Owen: Live in Michigan The twins are almost 2 years old, real characters, and keep both parents very busy. Denise teaches high school part time and Bryan owns and operates a major sports facility (indoor soccer,etc.).

Debra: Doing well in her consulting job. Bought a house in Sacramento and is learning how to fix things and do yard work. I told her she should have been helping me a long time ago and this would all be much easier. Her comment is she can hire it done for a lot less stress. Just got back from a trip to Brazil and loved it. She is not sure whether she is prepared for all the chaos of Christmas. (A lot like her dad).

Jill, Jerry, Gabriella (10) Sophia (4) & Joseph (2): Reside in Salinas. The children keep Jill very busy. She is a crafter, gardener and Longenberger representative in her spare time. Jerry owns and operates several farm industry businesses in Salinas, Heron, CA, and Yuma, AZ areas.

Mayling: 12 years old and runs our house. I am a little miffed at her for not writing this year's Christmas letter after all her training.

We have added a large room to our Sequim house so we now have plenty of room. If you are in the vicinity please stop by and visit. We are all well and happy. You are in our thoughts often and we hope the new year will be your best ever.

Love, Gill, Carol & Mayling

Sophia (4)

Gabriella (10)

Joseph (2)

Joshua & Owen (2)

2003

HAPPY HOLIDAYS

12 December 2003

I've taken pen in hand this year as Gill is taking another sabbatical. Even with the world somewhat in a turmoil our family has had a good year. We pray that 2004 brings the world a more peaceful situation and safety to our military members everywhere.

Gill suffered a mild a heart attack last January but with a stent and medication was back to his old self within a couple of days. He enjoyed his golf (4 handicap) and racquetball but he is now in rehab after rotator cuff surgery in November. Underfoot all day everyday and I can't wait for him to be out playing again.

In October we attended Gill's Coast Guard Academy 40th reunion in New London, CT and really enjoyed meeting up with old friends and rekindling memories of our youth. We stopped in Detroit on our way and spent a week with Denise, Bryan and their twins (Joshua & Owen). It was a lot of fun watching two-year olds and being happy that raising children is for the young. Then we met up with Denis and Beverly Bluett in Easton, MD and filled up on blue crab and played some golf. On our way home we went to Cape May, NJ and spent a couple of days. I could hardly recognize the place. (We were stationed there (1969-1973.) We did the tourist thing and stayed on the beach and shopped in all the Victorian shops in Cape May. When we went to Wildwood beach it was soooo different. What a trip.

I am getting older but not slowing down. Still having some success in golf and really enjoying my garden and stained glass work. Staying healthy so I can take care of Gill and Uncle Bill (now 92 years old). I enjoy volunteer work, church and visiting the kids and grandkids as often as I can. Life is good.

Debra is still in Sacramento doing consulting work. Has her own home and enjoying ownership and a place to call her own. It certainly has its ups and downs but she is happy.

Jill, Jerry, Gabby, Sophia and Joseph are still in Salinas and keep very busy. They are looking forward to moving into a new home after the first of the year.

All is well. We hope you have a Very Merry Christmas and a Happy New Year.

Fondly,   Gill & Carol

2004

Merry Christmas and Happy New Year

We hope 2004 was a good year for all of our friends. For our many friends in Florida we wish a quick recovery.

Our year started off with the death of Uncle Bill. (92) He was a great asset to our family and will be sorely missed. He lived a long, good life. We had a nice family reunion with a Celebration of His Life.

Denise, Bryan, Joshua(4) and Owen (4) are still in Michigan and enjoying the antics of their twin boys. We only got to see them once this year but next year I hope it will be more frequently. They grow much too fast.

Debra is still enjoying home ownership and working hard in Sacramento. She is trying to help Governor Swarzenegger trim California's budget. She became engaged this year so maybe we will have a new son-in-law next year.

Jill, Jerry, Gabriella (12), Sophia (6) & Joseph (aka little Gill) (4) have moved into a beautiful new home in the Salinas foothills. They actually want us to stay longer so they have a bedroom with it's own bath just for us. All are doing well and keep very busy. We will see them for Christmas.

Gill is still playing a lot of golf. Shot a 68 last week and credited this success to a new belly putter. He still enjoys racquetball 2-3 times a week and helps me in the yard when I can catch him. We did a lot of fishing this year and caught some nice salmon. We have a new tradition now with taking Gabby (granddaughter age 12) to Seiku about 50 miles west of Sequim, for a week of fishing in July. We have a great time. The other grandchildren only get a day trip until they get older. Gill didn't have any operations or any other medical surprises for me this year so I feel really blessed.

I spend my time playing a lot of golf, gardening, stained glass and started a genealogy search. Do volunteer work for my church and I enjoy the fellowship with other Christians. This year was a year of blessings. Denise, Debra, Jill, Sharon (my sister) and I all took a cruise to Alaska. We are still amazed at how fun it was for all. We went whale watching, dog sledding, helicopter ride, float plane ride with a bear hunt (no bears found) and a Skagway train ride. What a blast. It was a miracle to get all of us together for the same week. I was really impressed with my son-in-laws for taking charge of their respective house holds while their wives went off to play.

Maulina is still is still the boss of our house. She turned 14 this year and has slowed down considerably. She is almost blind and has selective hearing. We have become her seeing eye people.

Well I must close for now and get this in the mail. Have a Very Merry Christmas or Happy Hanukah and especially a happy, healthy New Year.

Gill & Carol

2006

16 December 2006

Dear Friends and Family,

The past year was a good, busy but slightly different from the norm. I'll try to explain: It started off with a January trip to Florida to visit Gill's sister and her family in Sarasota and then a visit to Denis and Beverly Bluetts (oldest CGA roommate) We did the usual things: sightsee, golf, dinners, wine, the works, great time lots of fun. Thanks for the memories...

In April, I and all the daughters went to Las Vegas to celebrate Jill's 35th birthday. The girls might have overdid it once or twice during our three days visit but remember what happens in Vegas stays in Vegas.. And as far as I'm concerned that rule makes a lot of sense.

We have all grown somewhat accustomed to Gill's annual need for attention via the medical surgery route (i.e., rotator cuff both shoulders, two knee, and a minor heart attack) but this year's stab for additional recognition was way past the limit. In April, Gill was rushed to the ER with a major staph infection which ended up just below his right knee. After running temperatures as high as 105F, four operations, and 14 days in the hospital the doctors had managed to save his life, his leg, but not his comb over (oh well, two out three isn't bad). I spent the next 2 months nursing, waiting on him, and giving him intravenous antibiotics every 8 hours while he complained about having to watch Oprah & Doctor Phil. Then 6 months of therapy/daily trips to the gym for strengthening/learning to walk again and old baldy is now back to his beloved racquetball. I call it a miracle! Gill's only comments, besides being very thankful, are: (1) if you have a choice skip any type of staph infection and (2) based on the measured average daily growth rate his new comb over will be ready for public viewing by Homecoming 2008.

In June my sister (Sharon) and I traveled to Colorado to reconnect with our family roots. I have been actively involved in genealogy research for a few years and this was the perfect field trip. We investigated and visited family in such places as Lakewood, Longmont, Cripple Creek, Victor, Leadville, Rifle, and Denver. Bet you haven't heard of all of them places. (By the way, I have also tried to investigate Gill's family roots but have run up against roadblocks from INS, IRS, FBI, etc. etc.. I really think somewhere back there the early Goodman was under the witness protection program.)

We spent the summer playing with daughter Jill and her children (Gabby, Sophia and Joey) here in Sequim. River rafting, bicycling, and other fun stuff took up most of the time and resulted in little time left for gardening, golfing, and other hobbies. Gill kept his boat at the dock in Seiku (about 60 miles west of Sequim) so he could jump in the car and be salmon fishing in 90 minutes. He sure enjoys his fishing. (peace and quiet)

Other family news: Daughter Denise (husband Bryan and twin sons Owen and Joshua) still reside just outside Detroit. They were here for a week in April.

Daughter Debra, (unattached), living/working in Sacramento. She got away for Memorial Day weekend to visit us

Daughter Jill, with the aforementioned crew living in Salinas, CA.

Newest addition to our immediate family is a cute, smart little Shih Tsu puppy appropriately named Mayling, (The Third) A blessing.

Pending trip: For the week between Christmas and thru New Years we have rented a house at South Shore Lake Tahoe. Rental is big enough for all the kids and grandkids and close enough for skiing, skating, gambling, (and racquetball) at Heavenly Valley Ski Resort. I hope to get a lot of good pictures of the younger group skiing. I will be happy to put my feet up, sip a hot toddy, and watch the fun.

Have a wonderful holiday season, stay well, and we hope to see you next year...

2007

December 2007

Gill and I wish all our family & friends a Merry Christmas and a Happy New Year.

May the spirit of Christmas remain with you throughout 2008.

For us 2007 started out great with a trip to the Lake Tahoe area. All the grandkids learned to ski and loved the tubing/ice skating. We had good weather and a lot of laughs. I was the official photographer and made an album for each family. We were amazed at how quickly the kids learned to ski. They were on the big runs by the third day. Everyone had so much fun.

In June, I became very ill and the emergency room personnel did not know what was wrong. I was sent home for more testing. At the end of three days they still could not determine the cause of my severe stomach pain. I then gave them two choices; they could either shoot me or go in and find out what was causing so much pain. They thought about shooting me but finally decided on exploratory surgery. Low and behold, it was a ruptured appendix and peritonitis had set in. I was in the critical care unit for 5 days and the hospital for nine. Because of the threat of infection they left the wound open to heal from the inside out. The wound had to be cleaned and the dressing changed twice a day at home by Dr.Gilly. (His bedside manner is a little rough but technically he knows medicine.) After nine weeks it was still not healed, so back to the hospital to clean up an abscess. That resulted in another month of open wounds and healing. Finally after 4 months I was out and about again. Dr. Gilly did a great job but was very happy to give up his responsibilities when I got well.

I played golf for the first time in late October and now have all my strength back. The whole ordeal was a time of letting go for me, the yard, the house & golf. I learned to be thankful in all situations. At first I wasn't completely comfortable putting my health and well being in Gill's hands but I don't know what I would have done without his help. I have decided I would rather be the caregiver.

We had many visits from family. Gabby, (eldest granddaughter) came in July and took over my care so Gill could go fishing for a few days in Seiku, (a fishing town about 60 miles west of Sequim). Debra came to watch movies with me and visit. In August, my sister came to take care of me after the second surgery, while Gill took off on another 3 day fishing trip. Sharon really helped get my yard in shape. What a blessing. In September Denise, Bryan, Joshua and Owen came for a week of fishing and visiting.

All of our family is doing well and I pray it stays that way. There has been way too much drama in 2007.

We (and Debra) are heading to Michigan for Christmas this year. Denise is busy making plans for a perfect Christmas celebration. We can hardly wait. We will miss Jill, Gabby, Sophia and Joseph as they could not get away from Salinas this year. Jill has bought a gift shop and makes specialty baskets so this is a very busy time of year for her. I took a quick trip to see them in November.

We will also be taking a trip to Hawaii in January with some friends of ours. We plan to visit many golf courses and some of the old familiar places.

Mayling III, our favorite little Shih Tzu, was my watch dog and constant companion during the long recuperation period. She is such a love and the smartest Shih Tzu west of the Mississippi.

May the Lord bless and keep each one of you safe, happy and healthy in the coming year.

Love, Carol (Gill & Mayling III)

2008

Dear Family & Friends

2008

We wish you all a very Merry Christmas and a Happy New Year. We hope that 2009 will bring a new awakening, and a change in the economic conditions, and a healthy, happy year.

Here on the homefront, 2008 has been the best year for quite a while: our health has been close to perfect (not bad for two old farts), fun vacations were taken and Sequim activities kept us busy and contented. A quick rehash of 2008's activities/vacations:

December 2008 - Holiday season in Michigan visiting Bryan, Denise and the twins (Joshua & Owen age 7).

Denise, Josh, Owen, Bryan
Denise, Debra, Carol
Josh & Owen

January- Spent a lovely week living on a beach in Hawaii. Lots of sun, golf and good food. (Note Baldy's surfing picture below.)

February - Couples golf tournament in Mesquite, Nevada (Should have won low gross but Baldy's putting went the same way his hair did.)

April - Easter in Salinas, CA visiting Jill and the grandchildren (Gabby 16, Sophia 10, Joey 7).

October - New London, CT for the 45th year reunion of the USCGA Class of 1963. (No sleep, a lot of old sea stories, and maybe a liver transplant now required.) Then we spent a week watching the leaves change in all the New England states (loved Boston, the Maine coast and the truly spectacular fall colors). Reconnected with some of Baldy's East Coast relatives (the ones that are still talking to him.) Got much info for Carol's genealogy research. Sidelight: While driving thru upstate NY visited Woodstock - missed the action 40+ years ago but did the town this time. Spent the day walking around town hearing Janis Joplin in my head. Instead of some LSD and a doobie we had a vanilla ice cream cone..... Damm what fun!!! Now we can say "We were at Woodstock when.....".

Two more trips to CA. One for a wedding reception for Carol's nephew and a combined trip to Disneyland.

November - A trip to help Gabby celebrate her 16th birthday.

December - Off to Sacramento to visit Debra and then to Salinas for Christmas with the aforementioned grandkids.

Life here in Sequim continues in its own quaint little way: Gilly into golf, racquetball, salmon fishing and rooting for his beloved NY Giants. Carol keeps busy with gardening, stained glass, golf, scrapbooking and rooting for her beloved church. (Our van now has two perfectly arranged back gate stickers: "JESUS SAVES:" and directly below "NY GIANTS". How about that Cowboy fans!!!

Again Happy Holidays...

Love, Gill, Carol & Mayling

Joey, Gabby, Gill, Sophia

Gabby

Gill Surfing

Gill at Woodstock

Grandkids showing love

2009

We wish you all a very Merry Christmas and Happy New Year... We hope that 2010 will bring a move toward greater worldwide peace, our country's continuing economic recovery, and a healthy, happy year for all our friends.

For us 2009 has been the best year in recent memory: good health, fun vacations, and many Sequim activities to keep us busy and content. I continue to be active with golf, gardening, and a host of arts/craft endeavors. Gill wastes his time chasing salmon, golf, lots of racquetball, and monitoring my church activities. (Upon meeting my favorite church Elder for the first time our boy observed that the gentleman looked so young and seriously inquired; "Are you like a junior Elder or an Elder in training?" and then "How old are you really?" End of conversation.)

January - Spent two weeks in Hawaii with Sequim friends and played lots of golf. It was nice to get away from last winter's odd Seattle weather (i.e., snow/cold temps/wind).

April – Back to Hawaii again for Debra's destination wedding to Derek Burk. Without a doubt, the social event of the year attended by 35 or so family and friends. The wedding ceremony was held on the same Kailua beach that Debra partied on as a bright and personable juvenile delinquent. It is amazing that none of the local police officers recognized her or her sisters (or her father, for that matter). Anyway it was a lovely week topped off by a perfect wedding. (The lucky couple then honeymooned in Bakersfield and Fresno.)

September – Attended Gill's 50th high school reunion in Mamaroneck, NY. First time he had seen any of his classmates since 1961. The weekend events were really quite informative and enjoyable. It was amazing but nobody had any open wounds or bad words to say about our boy. The first night's cocktail party was highlighted when he went up to an old acquaintance named Mary and told her she looked exactly the same. She then said "But you never thought I looked good!" I just shook my head when our boy responded with "But at least you don't look any worse." Silver tongued and one smooth guy! No wonder he was a 27-year old virgin when I met him.

While in New York area I took the opportunity and met an Aunt on my mother's side for the first time and reconnected with a cousin I hadn't seen in over 50 years. We shared stories and lots of pictures.

December – Spent the Christmas season with Debra/Derek in Sacramento and Jill/Grandkids in Salinas. Nice, quiet (?), quality family time... (Nothing quite as wonderful as preteens and teenagers.) We survived and had a very enjoyable time.

Hope to reconnect with one and all in 2010. If somehow we miss seeing you in person, please know you are in thoughts... We hope 2010 is the best year ever for you and yours!!!

Carol & Gill

2010

2010

We wish you a very Merry Christmas and a Happy New Year... We hope that 2011 will bring a move toward greater worldwide peace, our country's continuing economic recovery, and a healthy, happy year for all our friends.

For us 2010 has been a very good year: good health, fun vacations, and many Sequim activities to keep us busy and content. I continue to be active with golf, gardening, and a host of arts/craft endeavors. Gill wastes his time chasing salmon, golf, rooting for the NY Giants, and lots of racquetball.

Again we did our annual Hawaiian vacation. While on Oahu we met up with Coast Guard friends, played golf, and took surfing lessons. Needless to say, surfing is a lot of work for such a short ride. We decided we were too old for such a sport and next year we are going to try paddle surfing (on calm waters). We took a short side trip to Kauai and spent a few days site seeing.

In August, I went to Monterey to celebrate my 50th high school class reunion. I hardly recognized anyone. While in Monterey I had a lot more fun being with my grandkids.

I made a side trip to Sacramento to attend Debra's BABY SHOWER.

Yes, Debra had a beautiful baby girl October 27th. Her name is Lola Mikell Burk and she weighed in at 7 lbs 7 ozs. We are so thrilled for Debra and Derek. I spent 3 weeks with them and two of them were waiting for Princess Lola to arrive. She is such a good baby, and so cute. It has been 10 years since our last grandchild was born so it was fun to be around a new baby once again

Debra, Derek (& Lola) are in Sacramento and most of the time enjoying the experience of being new parents. Debra was allowed a 3-month maternity leave so that gives her time to adjust to her new mommy schedule.

Denise, Bryan, Joshua (10), Owen (10) are still living in Michigan. The boys are true sportsmen. They play soccer, baseball, football, and love to fish.

Jill, Sophia (12), Joseph (10) are still in the Monterey area and getting ready to move into yet another new house.

Gabriella, our oldest grandchild graduated from High School and in November had her 18th birthday. Where does the time go? She is off to college in Sacramento this month. Her goal is to eventually go into the Peace Corps.

Tomorrow Captain Baldy and I are headed off to California to spend Christmas with kids & grandkids.....

May peace and the Christmas spirit be with you in 2011,

Gill and Carol

2011

We wish you all a very Merry Christmas and Happy New Year. We hope that 2012 will bring a greater worldwide peace, economic recovery, and a happy year for all our friends.

For us 2010 has been a year filled with highs and lows…

First the lows: In the Spring, Carol was diagnosed with Breast Cancer and has spent the rest of the year going thru surgical procedures and then an aggressive chemo routine.. After six months of not so good times she is now on the upswing: gaining energy/weight, starting to grow hair, etc., etc. ready to attack 2012 with new found vigor. She said this experience has had some good aspects; she got to reconnect with all daughters who came to help, learned first hand the benefits of medical marijuana, and got to disregard anything her husband said citing a phenomenon known as "chemo brain".

Now for some highs:
- BC (before cancer) - Spent three weeks in Hawaii with Sequim friends and played lots of golf. It was nice to get away from last winter's Sequim weather.
- Carol's hearing problem corrected with a state-of-the-art hearing aid. The effect on our marriage was evident during the first week when Carol said something profound regarding the present national political situation. Gill, as he had been doing for decades, muttered under his breath "Oh bulls***, you dumb broad". For the first time in 20 years Carol heard him and went ballistic. Just proves that technology doesn't always make for a better, smoother marriage.
- All daughters are presently doing great. Of course, they should be, considering they are middle aged and have had a multitude of "life experiences". And yes, I do know their names: Denise, Debra, and Jill.
- All eight grandkids are growing and doing wonderfully. And no, I do not remember all their names. What I do know is that some of them are loud, unruly, potty mouthed, and ill behaved. Those take after Carol and her side of the family. The other gaggle of grandkids are polite, determined, articulate, and disciplined. Those are known throughout the family as Little Gillys or Gillettes.
- Mai Ling , our Shih Tsu, is still as treasured as ever. Gill considers her another daughter; not quite as good looking, slightly more hairy, nearly as intelligent, and certainly less mouthy/opinionated than the other three..

And now for the most important highlights: Although Carol doesn't give a fat rat's fanny, this year's salmon fishing was the best in a decade; caught five kings over 30 pounds. And best of all, after years of getting real close Gill finally shot his age. No, Carol, not bowling, not miniature golf, but real golf. Bucket list complete.

Hope to reconnect with one and all in 2012. If somehow we miss seeing you in person, please know you are in our thoughts. We hope 2012 turns out to be the best year ever. We thank God for all our blessings and one of them is your friendship.

Carol & Gill

2012

2012

We wish you all a very Merry Christmas and Happy New Year. We hope that 2013 will bring greater worldwide peace, continued economic recovery, and a very happy year for all our friends.

For us 2011 has been a year filled with lots of highs and very few lows:

Carol spent the first part of the year getting back to her BC (before cancer) old self; gaining energy/weight, growing hair, playing golf, committee meetings and such. The social event of the year was her 70th Birthday Party in August when all kids, grandkids, other relatives, and local friends gathered in Sequim. It was a grand party which was highlighted by a slide show of pictures (put together by her daughters) showing Carol from her childhood to the present. Damn, if we all didn't look better back then, but it did bring back a host of great memories.

I'm doing the same old stuff: golfing, salmon fishing, racquetball (but with a new twist – left handed since right shoulder rotator cuff tears/arteries have become an inoperable problem.).

Now for some highs and thoughts:
   - Last February spent three weeks in Hawaii with Sequim friends and played lots of golf..
   - All daughters are doing great. They still reside where we left them off in last year's letter.
   - All eight grandkids are doing wonderfully. It is a pleasure watching them grow up.. My favorite part is when their parents relate over the telephone how screwed up the grandkids are, note their disrespectful side, how uncontrollable, bad manners, etc.. You get the idea.. I just sit and giggle.. I think I said exactly the same thing 30+ years ago about my kids that they are saying now about their kids.. The Full Circle.. It is a beautiful thing..
   - May Ling , our Shih Tsu, is more treasured then ever. Gill considers her another daughter; as good looking, hairy, at least as intelligent and mouthy/opinionated as the other three..

When I showed Carol a draft of the above, she said "Is that all? What kind of Christmas letter is a couple of paragraphs? Give them more even if you have to write about the 'situation'." Well alright, here goes: It all began when I took on Bucket List, Item #22. Since I never believed losing 50+% of one's hair should preclude anyone from looking stylish I started to grow my remaining hair out to complete #22; a samurai warrior style ponytail. My big mistake was not asking Carol's permission (regardless of what you might think, she is very controlling) and when she realized what was going on she came up with comments such as: "You look like a moron!" If I wanted to marry a hippie, I'd have gone to the Monterey Jazz Festival or Woodstock in 1967!" I took that stuff for about a month before retorting with the likes of: "Your spiked hairdo reminds me of a buzz cut with peaks!" and "What are you? A British punk rocker ubersenior division!" This went on and on until a friend tired of hearing all the noise suggested we go to marriage counseling. I said great since that was Bucket List Item #24 and I could then complete two for one, so to speak. As usual, Carol monopolized the first hourly counseling session relating everything I had done wrong in the last 46 years. I was ready for the second session (I had a long list of Carol's faults) but before I could let go the counselor ask me "In your opinion, when did it all start to go wrong? After some thought, it came to me and I said; "About 15 years ago when we stopped going out dancing twice a week.". He said "Well gracious dear, start dancing again". Carol agreed immediately.. Well to make a long story short. We are now back to our previous routine of going out dancing religiously twice a week, every week!! Carol goes out on Tuesdays and I go out on Fridays. Isn't it great when a negotiated settlement works out for everyone.. Win Win…

Hope to reconnect with one and all in 2013. If somehow we miss seeing you in person, please know you are in our thoughts. We hope 2013 turns out to be the best year ever.
We thank God for all our blessings and one of them is your friendship. Stay healthy and safe!!
                              Gill & Carol

2013

2013

We wish you all a very Merry Christmas and Happy New Year. We hope that 2014 will bring worldwide peace, a functioning health care program, and a happy year for all our friends.

For us 2013 has been a year filled with lots of highs and no lows/regrets...
First, the personal updates:

Carol is doing great. Getting stronger with each passing day. Involved in golf, church groups, computer projects, and her gardening.. Intends to get serious about her golf game in 2014, starting with mucho practice sessions during our forthcoming Hawaiian trip next month and ending with a very competitive effort to win back her "gross" Club Championship next August..

I'm still doing the same old things: golf, salmon fishing, racquetball (back to right handed) and a new one – pickleball. All body parts necessary for those activities are hanging in there.

- All three daughters (& sons-in-law) and the nine grandchildren doing wonderfully. With my limited age-related retention ability it is impossible to keep up with all their doings but based on what I have overheard they are all now out of jail, all the house foreclosures have been suspended, and grand-daughter Lola (age 3) has been reinstated in Montesori School after serving her 2-day suspension. (The story is that Little Princess Running Mouth's non-stop yak yak drove her teacher to the brink and school officials trumped up some unrelated charges to give everyone a few days respite.)
- Mai Ling , our beloved Shih Tzu, is still as treasured as ever. Without a doubt, the most intelligent and patient member of this household.

Now for some of the awesome highs:

- Bucket List Item #18 complete.. After 40+ years of waiting/watching we finally saw the 'green flash' for the first time. During our annual trek back to Hawaii in February, we were having drinks/pupus at the Honolulu Elks Beach Bar (our best-ever watering hole) when it happened much to the delight of the 50 or assembled patrons. Amazing!!!
- In October I returned to the scene of the crime to attend my 50th reunion at the Coast Guard Academy (New London, Conn). Since Carol was unable to attend (see next item), my roommate for the week was my all-time bff: Denis Bluett. He was my first roommate at the Academy 54 years ago, so it was like déjà vous all over again. (Although this time he was a little wider, but just like old times he still snores and is most flatulent.) The reunion was filled with seeing old friends, going to many many ceremonies (in a blazer/tie), embellishing on old sea stories, and cringing when someone started with "Remember the time you.......". (Damn it, I swear I didn't!!) Overall good fun and I'm glad I went.
- The reason Carol couldn't accompany me to the East Coast was she providing assistance for daughter Debra during the birth of her new baby girl. Gilomenia Mikell Burk was born 30 October and mother and "Little Gilly" are doing great. I can honestly say it is truly humbling to have a baby named for you. This honor has caused me to reflect on my many misdeeds of years past. Although, heaven knows, I certainly was never voted Parent-of-the-Year mostly due to absences caused by Coast Guard career commitments and my quest for the perfect golf swing. But given this second chance I intend to make amends by becoming a full-time mentor and providing guidance to Little Gilly as she tackles life's problems, especially during her formative teenage years. I promise to provide expert counseling for the following areas/issues: sensitivity training, deportment, to shave or not to shave for the Big Dance, evils of demon rum, dating etiquette, Absolute versus Grey Goose, and profanity as a conversational tool. I also wanted to include religious indoctrination on my To Do list but received word from both worldly sources and voices above that her parents and/or Carol are better suited for that subject. In conclusion, I'm just so proud.. You Go, Little Gilly!!

MeRRy ChriStMAS - Recently I redid my will to make sure everything goes along smoothly when I retire to the big golf course in the sky. After much consideration I decided to be cremated and have my ashes spread equally between Macy, Wal Mart and Home Depot parking lots. Then I'll be comforted in knowing my daughters will visit me at least twice a week.

Hope to reconnect with one and all in 2014. If somehow we miss seeing you in person, please know you are in our thoughts. We hope 2014 turns out to be the best year ever. We thank God for all our blessings and one of them is your friendship.

Carol & Gill

2014

We wish you all a very Merry Christmas and a Happy Healthy New Year. We hope that 2015 will bring peace throughout the land, a functioning Washington DC, and a wonderful year for all our friends.

For us, 2014 has been a year filled with lots of highs and one incredible low...

First, the highs:

- Carol is doing great. Involved in golf, church groups, PEO, computer projects, and gardening. Got very serious about her golf game (13 handicap) in 2014: Won both her Woman's Club Champion- ship (overall net) and the Senior Woman's Club Championship (overall gross). From my experience being overall gross is top the heap. I try to encourage her to be continually as gross as possible.

- All three daughters (& sons-in-law) and the nine grandchildren are doing wonderfully. Everybody is getting bigger and more mature. First, there is Denise(X) and Bryan plus the twins Owen and Joshua (13). Then Debra (X-2) and Derek plus Lola (4) and Mikell aka "Little Gilly" (1). And finally Jill (X-4) and Lon plus Sophia (16), Joey (13), Jack (14) and Lexi (10). Out on her own, working and going to college in Sacramento, is Gabby (22). If I do say so myself, a fine and upstanding group!

- Mai Ling , our beloved Shih Tzu, now age 8 is still a treasure. Without a doubt, the most intelligent and less gross member of this household.

- Until a few months ago I was a happy guy doing what I always did: golfing (6 handicap), racquetball, salmon fishing, etc. having a ball. Although only family and few close friends knew; I have battled depression at various times during the past 40 years. A few months ago, the "dark mood" came again and this time, I'm afraid, had significantly intensified to a degree that I had to seek professional help. So for the past few months I have been seeing a local psychologist to help me deal and not do anything rash. After a few sessions my shrink had identified the problem, which I had believed to be centered around Carol's constant nagging. But, lo and behold, and Thank the Lord, because I was contemplating getting rid of the Old Bitty to ease the pain, he said that was not the problem. He revealed there were other forces in play...... As many of you are aware, I'm a rabid NY Giant football fan since 1948 when my father took me to my first game in the old Yankee Stadium. What you don't know is at the end of each season for the past 40 years or so, I have been sending a letter to the owner (Mr. Mara & sons) giving them my expert opinion on all aspects of their team's operation, including coaches/players performance critiques, forthcoming draft choice possibilities, cheerleader selection criteria/uniform fitting requirements, etc.. (I usually get a warm and fuzzy reply from Mr. Mara stating something to the effect: "We appreciate your support/interest, now go p—ss off".) The Giants have been so bad for the past 2.5 years that this year's letter was sent mid-season and was 5 pages long ending with my suggesting he and I do a long lunch at Sardi's (a famous NYC watering hole) during which I'll help him think his way out of the horrible mess. Although I haven't heard from him yet, I'm sure I'll be off to the Big Apple as soon as the season ends. Then, and only then, will the "dark mood" lift and I'll be free again, free again..

Be advised: Next year's Christmas letter will feature, by popular demand, the Return of the Silver Castor Canadensis. To wet your appetite it will include true (honest I swear) stories such as: The time Carol dropped the only rent-a-car keys in the hotel toilet on the last morning of our Hawaiian vacation minutes before we were to leave for the airport. (How? Don't asked. I didn't.) In any case, not a problem you say, just fish them out.. OK, but these keys had a microchip inside and were clearly marked "Do Not Get Wet!!". Damn if the car didn't start up right away and we were able to skip town with no delay.

A postscript on my NY Giant babble noted above: I have recently changed my will by putting in the stipulation in that my pallbearers be six NY Giant players led by Eli Manning himself. This will positively ensure that it will be the last time a group of NY Giants players ever let me down.

Hope to reconnect with one and all in 2015. If somehow we miss seeing you in person, please know you are in our thoughts. We hope 2015 turns out to be the best year ever. We thank God for all our blessings and one of them is your friendship.

Gill & Carol

2015

December 2015

We wish you all a very Merry Christmas and a Happy Healthy New Year. We hope that 2016 will bring peace throughout the land, smooth/competent leadership from Washington DC, and a wonderful year for all our friends.

For us 2015 has been an interesting year: another whirlwind retirement year (In our previous life, how did we ever find time to work for a living.) In addition, we had a life-altering event that significantly strengthen my marriage and I lived thru one health problem of note.

More on those matters later, but first a file dump of family news:

 - Carol is doing great. No health problems except those associated with the normal aging process(?). Involved in golf, church groups, PEO, computer projects, and gardening. Still serious about her golf game (15 handicap). Won the Senior Woman's Club Championship.

 - All three daughters (& sons-in-law) and the nine grandchildren are doing wonderfully! But there appears to be an abnormal behavioral problem noted in our teenage grandkids. Thirty years ago all I had to do was observe/record the misadventures, bad decisions, and outright looney antics of my teenage daughters and the Christmas letter would effectively write itself. (By the way, God bless my daughters for their long ago daffy efforts to keep me and the whole world entertained.) But now when I call these same daughters and ask for some dirt regarding their teenagers for the Christmas letter, I get the following: "She is honor roll. He is President of the class/Captain of the football team/voted most likely to succeed. Stanford called yesterday offering a full ride for academics. Always in the books at least 4 hours a night. Drinks only organic yak urine. Blah, Blah, Blah.". So either I have been blessed with the most perfect, well behaved teenage grandkids or I'm not getting the full scoop. Hopefully, it is the latter. The only news worthy items I have regarding my teenage grandkids this year are: Sophia (17), inside linebacker for Palma HS, dislocated her shoulder during a successful goal line stand. Joey (15), 6'3" All County Cheerleader, broke his wrist when he was dropped from the top of the pyramid. I certainly hope all these teenagers have a more exciting, an eventful 2016.

- Mai Ling, our beloved Shih Tzu, now age 10, remains the quintessential doggie diva.

- Aside from the stuff noted below I am doing great with no major problems. My highlights for my year: caught a 40+ pound salmon (with witnesses on board), shot my age a couple of more times and won my golf club's Match Play Championship (good for a few c notes & a year's worth of bragging rights).

First, a rehash of the monumental event that without doubt strengthen, and probably saved, my marriage. As those that know me will attest, I have maybe just a few rough edges that could cause a minor glitch or two in a functioning marriage, but come on, to be fair, nothing major. That is why I could never understand the high volume of BS that ensued every time I forgot our anniversary or Carol's birthday. (Heck it was only about 50% of the time.) Well anyways, last June 16th I got ahead of the power curve and bought her a huge box of her favorite dark chocolates for our anniversary. When I gave her the gift that evening, I watched her jaw drop to floor, not because I actually remembered the anniversary but because she had forgotten. Although I was stunned at her first major slip up in 47 years of marriage, I kept my composure/stayed focused and let the following rip: "I knew you never loved me.", "You take me for granted.", and "I feel like nothing more that the houseboy around here." I kept this dialogue up steady for 2 weeks and then tapered off. But in her little mind she now knows that her major faux pas will never be forgotten and can be used as a trump card during any future arguments. God, I do love a gift that keeps on giving!

The health issue of note involves my right knee replacement done a month ago. Since this was my fourth major knee operation in the past 13 years I was fully aware of the procedures, protocols, scheduling, and rehab required. But unlike "normal" knee replacements, mine required clean out of past knee operations and the remnants of a major staff infection years ago. This has resulted in a much more painful rehab process which I countered by pouring on the prescribed painkillers. I knew this approach could potentially cause problems: I was worried not about addiction but rather a major stoppage issue. Because of my unblemished history of 6 minutes after I get up, 2 sips of coffee and a middy is launched, I am known throughout the Sequim area as "Captain Regular - Father of the Always Timely, Perfect Stool". (No Jill, we are not talking about you.) I took immediate corrective action by implementing the, tried and true, Gilly laxative geometric progression algorithm (i.e., one pill first night, 2 the second, 4 the third, 8 the fourth, till situation is resolved). This algorithm has never failed to produce results but the worry is, that if you get into the fifth day before the situation is resolved, the results could be catastrophic. Lucky for me, the afternoon of the third day was spent sitting down, you know where, contemplating whether this knee replacement was a good idea in the first place. Even more troubling was that night's 12-yard mad dash from a dead sleep, one legged on the walker, dragging the connected narcotic IV behind to a sudden but successful conclusion. Although Carol laughed till it hurt when I told her about it the next morning, if the situation is ever reversed I intend to be there with a video camera to record her mad 12-yard dash for an all-time YouTube video clip.

Gill & Carol

2016

15 December 2016

Merry Christmas and Happy New Year to all our friends and family -

This year has been a roller coaster. Up Down Up Down.

Denise, Bryan, Josh & Owen are still living in Michigan. They are involved in a major home remodel and lots of traveling. The boys (now almost 16) participate in numerous elite soccer leagues.

Debra, Derek, and daughters Lola (6) & Mikell (3) are living in Sacramento. They are both working full time. Derek has started his own business. The girls are growing so fast and are so cute.

Jill, Lon, Sophia, Joey, Jack & Lexi are in Salinas. Sophia will be graduating from High School this next year. Jack got his driver's license and Joey will be 16 in January. They are all growing up so fast and I can hardly believe how fun they all are. Gabby is attending Sacramento State and has already started the job of her dreams. She is a preschool teacher (Not daycare). She loves the little ones. We visited last February and took all grandkids paintballing. I told them I needed to shoot me some grandkids.

Gill recovered nicely from his knee replacement. He is playing racquetball, pickleball and golf. His athletic highlight this year was winning his golf club's Super Senior Gross Championship.

I am still involved in golf. My partner and I won the Member/ Member tournament this year. I didn't do as much work in my yard as I was not feeling very well. Church is still one of my favorite events. I was asked to give a testimony of some events in my life and I agreed to speak. My testimony is on YouTube when you get to YouTube, type in Carol Goodman's testimony.

In July, after many tests, I was diagnosed with Ovarian Cancer. The protocol was to have nine weeks of chemo to reduce the scope of the cancer, have surgery to remove as much cancer as possible and then follow up by nine more weeks of chemo. I had surgery on the 26th of October and we are now 1/3 the way thru the follow up chemo phase. I was most disappointed that I would not be able to go south for Christmas. I can't do Christmas without family. So all the daughters, husbands, and grandkids all decided to come up here for Christmas. They are figuring out the logistics of this trip. They are setting everything up as far as decorating the tree and meals. I can hardly wait to see them all.

I just finished my book. I wrote this book so my children and grandchildren will have the history of my parents, grandparents and my life. I have named the book "The Gift of Faith". My gift of faith has kept me going throughout the years with many challenges in my life. It is due to be published in 2017.

I hope 2017 is a great year for us all. Our nation needs us to become kinder to one another. There is way too much anger and animosity. Let's make next year the best.

With love,

Carol & Gill

See Reverse

Gill's Two Cents: As everybody is aware, I was blessed with a boatload of daughters and my first two grandchildren were female so, until recently, I never had a chance to pass on to my male offspring, the things that I had learned regarding the dating scene male/female interplay. Come on guys, haven't we all said, "If I knew then what I know now, I would have been the coolest Romeo ever". Well, during the last year, I got a chance to pass on that kind of important info since I now have four grandsons all about 16 or so. I started my mentoring with the grandson that has a beautiful, restored '66 Mustang, just like the one I had 50 years ago when I was a youthful bachelor Lieutenant. Young man, I said, "that car is an incredible chick magnet and there is no way you can screw this up!! So when you get the young lovely to the drive-in movie, try this approach......." He said "Whoa! What is a drive-in movie?" And then, "Why would my date and I want to watch the movie in a car when we could watch it at home with my parents on Netflix?" It is now obvious to me that whatever cool dating secrets I have will go to the grave with me. How things have changed!!

APPENDIX

EMAIL COMMUNICATION WITH ALICE AND FRIENDS

From: kmccarle <kmccarle@neo.rr.com>
To: Carol Goodman <cgoodman@olypen.com>
Sent: Wednesday, March 15, 2000 11:07 PM
Subject: Re: long time waiting...Michele's friend Kathleen

Dear Carol

I believe his name was deacon Paul. I did go to see Father Tony. He was a very special friend of my family and he helped me get through all the rough times. I still keep in touch with him through e-mail. I dug out my old journals and yearbooks to see if i could find anything that I had written about michele. I did find a space in my year book that I wrote about her to myself..."In memory of Michele. I will never forget you. We were the best of buddies, I miss you so very much. I love you. By Kathleen LaVallee." I couldn't believe they didn't dedicate a page to her memory either. I was really upset. I also found a page in my journal. I guess I started writing sometime after Michele went to be with God. This is what I wrote." March 12,1980 9:12pm. Just laying here on my bed thinking about Michele.I miss her so much. I could always talk to her like a sister and I could always trust her. God she was such a beautiful person, so pure, so innocent. Why did she have to die. Michele please forgive me for not getting to you in time. I need your smiling face to make me laugh the way you use to do. Someday we will see each other again....Watch over me, okay?"

I don't know if that helps you any. She never told me she was unhappy. We always use to laugh and giggle. Sometimes kids say things they really don't mean. I bet if she would have gone to her dads she would have been home to you in site of two weeks. I know she loved you and her family. I think she was just testing your love. We will all meet. I look forward to the day when I can tell her how much she meant to me. Also to tell my parents all the things I never said when they were alive. I said some hurtful things to my mother too.
I believe you and Michele had a very close relationship. If I remember correctly she said she could talk to you about anything. I wish I had felt that way about my mom. I did finally realize that I could talk to her about anything after my father died, but I wasted a lot of time.
I am so glad that we were able to connect. Please don't lose touch with me. I love hearing from you. Kathleen

-----Original Message-----
From: Carol Goodman <cgoodman@olypen.com>
To: Alice Vanni <aleka@fimg.net>
Date: Thursday, March 16, 2000 3:55 PM
Subject: Michelle

Dear Alice,
I am so pleased to hear you are well and happy. I have often wondered how you are and if you ever found peace in your life. I know for a long time you were in nothing but turmoil. I was given this

poem a long long long time ago and I knew it was for me. I wanted to share it with you because even though you feel responsible it was truly Michelle's time to go home. I always knew that and even though I missed her terribly I had enough faith to believe that God always has a plan for out lives.

I'll lend you for a little time
a child of Mine, He said.
For you to love the while she lives
and mourn for when she's dead
It may be six or seven years,
or twenty-two or three
But will you, till I call her back,
take care of her for Me?
She'll bring her charms to gladden you,
and should her stay be brief
You'll have her lovely memories
as solace for your grief.

I cannot promise she will stay,
since all from earth return.
But there are lessons taught down there
I want this child to learn.
I've looked the wide world over
in my search for teachers true
and from the throngs that crowd life's lanes
I have selected you.

Now will you give her all your love,
nor think the labor vain
Nor hate Me when I come to call,
to take her back again?
I fancied that I heard them say,
"Dear Lord, Thy will be done,
For all the joy Thy child shall bring,
the risk of grief we'll run.
We'll shelter her with tenderness,
we'll love her while we may,
And for the happiness we've known,
forever grateful stay,
But should the angeles call for her
much sooner than we've planned,
We'll brave the bitter grief that comes,
and try to understand.

Author Unknown

Having a child is the greatest learning experience in life. We never know true, unconditional love until we see that childs face. We are not in control of their destiny we are only to love and guide them the best we can. Gods teaching is all about love, foregiveness and faith in knowing he is in charge if we will get out of the way and let him do his work (in our lives and in others).
I am now on a new level of love with my Grandchildren. It is hard to believe that the love I feel for them is so powerful I am overwhelmed at times. Ask your mom. Being a grandparent is worth the time spent with unruly teenagers. Well I must close for now. I pray for a healthy second child and give your son a big kiss for me and let him know he is special. Fondly Carol Goodman

p.s. Your great Aunt kept in contact with me for a long time. Is she still around? How is your mom and dad?

Carol Goodman

From: Alice Vanni <aleka@fimg.net>
To: Carol Goodman <cgoodman@olypen.com>
Sent: Tuesday, March 21, 2000 1:22 PM
Subject: Aloha from Maui

Dear Carol:
I finally have a chance to respond to your letter last week. It's been crazy for me lately, both at work and home, so it's nice to catch my breath every now and then.

Thank you for sharing the poem with me. I do believe that as parents all we can do is provide a morally responsible, loving and nurturing environment for our children and hope they make it through their "growing years" to become responsible citizens. I believe true success for any parent is when your child comes to you and says "thanks mom & dad for all you've done for me"...I know I appreciate my parents for all they had to endure during my growing pains!

I've had some difficult times in the last 20 years, but feel very blessed for what I have and am always thankful to those in my life that gave me the benefit of doubt and provided me more chances than I probably deserved. It hasn't always been easy...I've always been the hardest on myself...but having the faith that I have now has helped me in so many ways. My belief is that events (challenges in our lives) do "happen for a reason", and all we can do is try to search out the positive aspect of the event and truly learn and grow from it -- not dwell on the negativity....the "oh poor me" syndrome. I finally figured that one out, but it took an awfully long time!

I am very happy and well! I have a great husband, Paul (10 years, this July), an incredible son (Matthew), and will add a daughter in August, the good Lord willing. I have finally found peace, thanks to the love and support of those around me. For so many years I tried to do it on my own...God kept trying to tell me it didn't have to be that way but, of course, I didn't pay attention. Now I do. Now that I've opened my heart to God, I understand that it's not humanly possible to do it all on my own. For this reason alone, I am at peace.

There isn't a day the goes by when I don't think of Michelle...in some way or another. I talk to her ALL the time, mainly at night when the stars are out. She has, and always will be, my guardian angel.

To answer your questions at the end of your letter; my great Aunt Jessie died in 1991; I wish I'd known her better. My mom and dad are doing great! My father finally "fully" retired in 1995. He now does volunteer work for Hospice and keeps busy with Matthew whenever he can. My mom is "semi-retired", and works as a Hospice Nurse, here on Maui. Quite the contrast to Labor and Delivery for 17 years, yet the similarities are there... They travel as much as they can, but are here on Maui most of the time in an ohana directly behind our house, believe it or not! It's great because Matthew has something that neither Paul nor I had...a relationship with his grandparents. I feel that Maui is one of the most beautiful places in the world to live and am grateful for it's beauty and warmth.

Thank you for your prayers and support.
Love and Aloha!
Alice

ABOUT THE AUTHOR

Carol Goodman is 74 years old. She lives in Sequim, Washington with her husband, Gill.

68165563R00099

Made in the USA
Lexington, KY
04 October 2017